The Lazy Person's Guide!

Quitting smoking

S0-ARM-748

Quitting smoking

Gillian Riley

Newleaf

Newleaf

an imprint of
Gill & Macmillan Ltd
Hume Avenue
Park West
Dublin 12
with associated companies throughout the world
www.gillmacmillan.ie

© Gillian Riley 2001
0 7171 3270 6
Design by Vermillion Design
Illustration by Emma Eustace
Print origination by Linda Kelly
Printed by ColourBooks Ltd, Dublin

This book is typeset in Rotis Semi-Sans 10pt on 13pt.

The paper used in this book comes from the wood pulp of managed forests. For every tree felled, at least one tree is planted, thereby renewing natural resources.

A CIP catalogue record for this book is available from the British Library.

5 4 3 2 1

CONTENTS

CHAPTER 1

THE LAZY GUIDE

You can stop smoking.

Yes, you.

Yes, smoking.

What's even better, it doesn't matter if you don't believe it. You don't need to start out convinced that you will stop, that it won't be unbearable torture and that after you've stopped your life will carry on much as before. You don't need to believe any of that at all.

In fact, it's much more likely you'll start out very unsure. Unsure whether or not you really can break free from cigarettes, what it will be like without them and even whether or not you really do want to stop in the first place.

If you are like most smokers, stopping smoking seems a huge, daunting challenge. It means stepping into the unknown, risking losing control. Losing control, perhaps, over your emotions, over your eating, over your sanity, over your daily life as you know it. If you are keen to quit, your fear of failure looms large. If it's not a big priority the risk of failing doesn't matter so much, but either way, setting a date to quit gets put off and put off.

Perhaps you've stopped before and you can remember just how nasty it was. Not only was it awful, but you failed as well. So you went through all that misery for nothing! Or perhaps you've noticed other smokers trying to stop, struggling with the bad temper, the weight gain and the feelings of loss and deprivation.

Or you've noticed other smokers who manage to stop for a while but always go back, again and again.

So, just consider this. What if there was a way to stop smoking and actually feel good about the whole thing? What if you actually felt better when you didn't smoke, more capable of dealing with your life, more on top of things in general? What if you didn't get irritable and didn't gain weight either? What if you didn't get depressed or miss cigarettes terribly? What if you enjoyed your social life just as much as when you smoked, even though your friends were still puffing away?

Well, it's all possible. Stopping smoking doesn't have to be a miserable experience, doomed to fail from the start. It's just that so many people make it more difficult than it really needs to be, even though they don't mean to. They make it more difficult by creating problems in the early stages after stopping. Problems that don't need to happen. And people make it more difficult by not understanding how to stay stopped in the long term. So they stop smoking but then they start again, and then they stop again, and then they start again. And then they stop again and then they start again. For many, it gets more and more difficult each time they stop, and it all takes a great deal of effort and much more mental energy and anguish than it needs.

This book is all about how you avoid these problems. It's about understanding a few crucial things that make all the difference between failure and success. So that, yes, quitting is a challenge and there is some difficulty involved, but you learn how to deal with that difficulty in a powerful way. And, if you understand some things, you succeed in the long term so that you don't need to keep going through the process of stopping over and over.

To begin with, it's best to expect that stopping smoking will take some time and effort, especially in the first couple of weeks and, if you handle it right, just a little bit of time later on. It won't be completely overwhelming and impossibly demanding, but it is something you need to pay some attention to and be careful about in the early stages.

Now let's think about this for a minute, because here you are reading a book about stopping smoking, so obviously you think that quitting might be a good idea. So, why wouldn't you go ahead and start getting to work with this technique, put a reasonable amount of effort into it and get the good results you want? It sounds so simple, but there is a real chance you'll leave this book lying around for a while ... and then one day you'll be tidying up and you'll put it on a shelf ... and maybe in a year or two you'll come across it and think that one day you'll use it to stop smoking. And that really is the big thing about stopping. It's doing it in the first place.

So. If you are ready to set a quit date now, go straight to the 'What you can do' section at the end of this chapter. If not, ask yourself why you aren't ready to stop. You may come up with one or more (or all!) of the following:

● *I know I'll fail, I'm such a hopeless case.* This is a very common stumbling block, because most smokers can't imagine themselves not smoking, so they assume they'll fail. This fear may be greater if you've never tried to quit before and have smoked for most of your life. Or if you've tried to quit but failed time and time again. Either way, you simply won't be able to see yourself succeeding – so don't even try! It's how almost every smoker starts out. You don't need to believe in your success in order to succeed. Just take things bit by bit and follow this book through and see what happens.

If you've tried many other methods, there's one glimmer of hope I can offer you right now: I guarantee that this technique is different from those you have tried before. Maybe, just maybe, you'll learn something here that makes the crucial difference for you this time. That's all you need to start with. Maybe. And the courage to try.

● *It's not a good time right now.* You could be right, especially if you're going through a time of great stress, unusual upheaval or emotional crisis. For example, if you have recently lost a loved one and are going through a period of grief and readjustment. Or when you need every bit of concentration, when sitting exams for example.

Sometimes it isn't the right time to stop because you don't want to take on too much at once. But be careful here, because smokers can ALWAYS find good excuses to keep on smoking just that little bit longer. So see if this very stressful situation is fairly short term, and find some way to remind yourself about stopping smoking when you think it will be over, so you can reconsider then. Put a date in your diary or a mark on your calendar and agree with yourself: OK, things are too crazy right now, but I'll go ahead and set a date to quit later on when things are more settled.

Of course you could be one of those people who are permanently stressed out, facing one crisis after another, either at work or at home or both. In this case, ask yourself if you don't mind going on smoking for as long as this lifestyle is likely to last – which could be for the rest of your life! If you do mind, then stopping smoking while all the crazy stuff is happening is going to be the way forward. You can do it, and this book will show you how.

- *I enjoy smoking; it's my only vice, my little treat, my only pleasure.* The problem, of course, is that it's a pleasure and a treat that costs you dearly. There's the financial cost and the cost to your health, the quality of your life and to your self-esteem. The more years you smoke, the higher these costs get.

  For most smokers, the sense of pleasure or satisfaction in smoking doesn't go away entirely, so don't wait until you wake up one morning and see no pleasure in smoking ever again. In most cases, this doesn't happen. Quitting smoking is the process of re-evaluating the cost versus the pleasure. It's about acknowledging the attraction of smoking and weighing it up against how destructive it is. This book will show you how to do that, step by step.

- *I felt so dreadful (or gained so much weight) last time I quit.* Some of the difficulty you may have experienced came from the physical changes your body went through when you stopped smoking. These can be alleviated by using some form of Nicotine Replacement Therapy (such as gum or patches) and/or the anti-depressant used to help smokers quit called bupropion (the current commercial name is Zyban). However, part of the difficulty you may have experienced before came from your attitude, the way you were thinking about it. If you change that – and that's what this book's about – much of the difficulty evaporates.

● *I might succeed – which means I'll never smoke again!* It's worth pointing out that success can be every bit as frightening as failure. It really is best to remember that you just don't know how things will turn out, and you don't need to know. Maybe you'll stop and maybe you won't. Maybe you'll stay stopped and maybe you won't. Just give it a go, and see what happens.

WHAT YOU CAN DO

■ *Read through this book before you stop,* so you can get a sense of what it's all about. If you want to, go on smoking while you read it. Please don't feel guilty about smoking while you read – that's why you're reading this book! First of all you're going to understand the problem, and then you can put it into action. Think of it as looking at a map before you start a journey. You see where you're going, how to get there and what problems you might run into on the way. Then, you take the journey.

If you've already stopped, by the way, that's OK. It's still a good idea to read the book, because it will help you to stay stopped. You don't need to go back to smoking in order to follow this technique correctly. All it may take is a little course correction which will help you to stay stopped this time.

■ *Get involved.* This book is a 'Lazy Person's Guide' because it's dead easy to follow. I'll take you through the steps you need to take and be very clear about how to deal with every problem you could meet on the way. But this doesn't mean you can get away with being lazy and have it all done for you! This book provides you with tools for you to use. They are excellent tools for the job – but they will only work if you use them. If you don't use them, just the same as when you leave any tool lying around on a shelf, you don't get the job done. So that's the part that is very much up to you.

■ *Keep it private.* When you are ready to set a quit date, prepare yourself by keeping it to yourself as much as possible. Don't go around telling people you're stopping and don't talk about what you are doing and how you are feeling. When you start talking about it you get other people involved. Later on they could make very unhelpful comments, even though they may be trying to help you. If nobody knows you're stopping, nobody will talk to you about it. If anyone notices you're not smoking (it's amazing how many people *don't* notice!) and they ask you about it, just say something vague, such as, 'I'm trying to cut down' or 'I may have one later on' and try to change the subject.

■ *Get some support.* The one exception to keeping it all to yourself would be in involving one person who is going to support you in stopping smoking, or in joining a group, perhaps at your local doctor's surgery, hospital or health centre.

If you choose a friend to support you, make clear agreements before you stop about what this support will be. Is your friend willing to take phone calls from you? Or will they call you? How often? Do you plan to meet at regular times to talk about how things are going?

If this is someone you see often, it's best to have agreed times to talk about quitting, rather than just bringing it into conversations at any time. You can plan these support sessions as you go along. To start with, you may want to talk to your support person often, say every day or every other day. After the first week you may feel more confident and need them less.

One word of advice about this support person. If you have someone in your life who very much wants you to stop smoking, who has even been putting pressure on you to stop, this is not the person who would be good to support you. Pressure is the last thing you need, because it can make you want to rebel. The way a smoker rebels, in case you don't know, is by lighting up a cigarette.

You need to find a support person who doesn't mind whether or not you smoke, so that they can help *you* to find what's right for *you*. They will listen to you and help you to understand what's going on in the way you are thinking about smoking and stopping smoking, so it's essential for them to read this book too, so they know what you're doing.

■ *Decide on what prescription aids you want to use.* You may want to ask your doctor or practice nurse about Nicotine Replacement Therapy (NRT) and/or Zyban. More about these in Chapter 7.

■ *Know your reasons for stopping.* Some people approach quitting with only a vague sense that it's something they are supposed to do. It's much more powerful to have as clear a vision as possible of the ways in which your life will improve after you've stopped.

Ask yourself, '*Why* do I want to quit smoking?' This is your motivation and it's a crucial key to your success.

It could be that you don't feel totally enthusiastic about quitting to begin with. It could be that you have mixed feelings, not at all sure you want to stop – and maybe not at all sure you *can* stop. This is a fine place to start. You are feeling some conflict, and that's your starting point. For some people, motivation about not smoking develops slowly over time, and there's nothing wrong with that.

■ *Make a note for yourself* and think of it as a message to yourself in the future, reminding yourself of the difference between smoking and not smoking in your life. You could start off with, 'When I'm a smoker ...' and 'When I've stopped smoking ...'

List everything you can think of, for example, 'When I'm a smoker I cough a lot in the mornings', and 'When I've stopped smoking I feel proud of myself.' Add to this list as you go on. After you've stopped, you may see something you like about not smoking which surprises you, so write that down too.

This list is for your eyes only, so keep it somewhere private. And keep it somewhere you can easily find it and may even come across it when you're looking for something else, so it can remind you as time goes on.

■ *Make it selfish.* Whenever you think about your reasons for stopping, find reasons that matter to you and only you. As much as you can, make quitting something you are doing to please yourself, rather than to please other people.

This can make a huge difference, especially if you're the sort of person who does a lot for others. You may regard smoking as the one thing you do for yourself, that a cigarette is your reward for all the hard work you do every day. If this is the case, the last thing you want to do is to stop smoking for the sake of others, because this makes it one more act of self-sacrifice in a life of service for other people. When it comes to stopping smoking, that's simply not going to work.

Of course you can't make the needs of others go away. If you have children who are asthmatic, you can't forget the fact that they will benefit if you stop smoking. Or if you have a partner who hates you smoking, you know they will be delighted when you stop. What's going to help you, though, is if you put these things to one side in your mind and focus on how quitting will benefit you. Will you have more energy? Better breathing? More money? Greater self-esteem? It's these things that will make all the difference, because then quitting is a gift you give to yourself instead of a sacrifice you're making. Then it's something you're more likely to want to keep.

■ *Start to think about when you're going to quit.* Perhaps you want to choose a special date, a birthday or an anniversary. I stopped smoking on November 5th, and enjoy a very private celebration every year.

If you aren't ready to think about stopping yet, just continue reading. The things you read about over the next few chapters can help you get to that point by removing some of the obstacles in the way.

How I Quit: Gillian

Here is something about my own experience of quitting. The rest of the 'How I Quit' sections which follow each chapter are from clients of mine. I've chosen clients who at the time had quit smoking fairly recently. Being closer to the initial process of quitting, I think their stories will be more relevant to you.

I stopped smoking about 20 years ago and for 16 of those years I led seminars, teaching people how to quit. 20 years is a long time, but the day I stopped smoking I didn't have the slightest idea I'd stay stopped for that long. I wouldn't have been able to imagine it. How could I? I just thought I'd take it one day at a time and see what happened. That's really all I could do and in a way it's all I'm still doing. I love not smoking, though, so I don't see myself going back to it. Obviously as far as my work is concerned, it would be a very good idea if I didn't smoke now; but much more important is the benefit to me personally.

My number one benefit from quitting is energy. I know that some people aren't affected by smoking in this way but for me, smoking drained my energy dramatically. I used to feel sleepy in the afternoons and could quite easily have taken a nap every day around 4 or 5 o'clock in the afternoon. I think the energy you have to get you through the day is so important, because that's your life.

The interesting thing to me is that I didn't know it was my smoking that was causing my low energy until after I'd stopped. Suddenly, I had more than enough energy to get through the day and only then did I realise it was all to do with smoking. And 20 years later I still have more than enough energy to get me through the day and to do anything I want to do, whether it's work or play. I hate running out of energy and that's the main reason I haven't gone back to smoking. The thing is, I've remembered this detail about energy for all these years. It's because I've made a special effort to remember it. I can't remember a lot about what my day-to-day life was like 20 years ago, but I've deliberately remembered that, because it's my main motivation to stay stopped.

For me the bottom line has always been this: so OK, maybe I could have one cigarette and get away with it. But why take the risk? For one cigarette, which is going to last maybe ten minutes, I might be throwing away the chance to stay free from smoking. What if smoking that one cigarette meant I went back to smoking and continued smoking for the rest of my life? It really is possible. Maybe I'd stop again, but what if I didn't? So far, I haven't thought that one cigarette was anywhere near worth that risk.

CHAPTER 2

TAKE THE ANGUISH OUT OF QUITTING

Have you ever been forced to do something you didn't want to do? It's a nightmare, isn't it? For everyone, our freedom is so important that we'll do anything to preserve it and we react strongly if it's taken away. Even if we were made to do something quite pleasant, to watch a movie for example, we would hate it if we were taken to the cinema by force and tied into the seat so we couldn't leave. Maybe we would have enjoyed this movie, but when we don't have our own freedom of choice in the matter, we just get angry and resentful. We would plan escape and plot revenge. Maybe we'd try going along with it for a while, but if this kind of coercion went on and on in our lives, and if we didn't rebel, our spirits would finally be broken. Then depression and low self-esteem set in. Loss of freedom is one of the very worst things that can ever happen to us.

If you have someone in your life who has been trying to get you to stop smoking, I expect you can see how this is relevant. Whether it's a parent, a partner, a friend or society in general who is trying to make you quit, the usual response is to light another cigarette rather than submit to their pressure. But this isn't quite the point I'm wanting to make. Whether you have someone else pressuring you to stop or not, the real problem lies not in someone else's nagging, but in *your own*.

Almost all smokers, when they start to think about quitting, begin to think along the lines of: 'I have to stop smoking' and 'I can't go on smoking.' Then, when they stop: 'I can't let myself fail' and even, 'I mustn't ever smoke again.' They try to stop by threatening themselves and by thinking they have no choice in the matter. So what happens? Even though it's you who's doing the forcing, you react as if you were no longer free to smoke, as if you had been made to stop.

This creates two kinds of problems with quitting. The first problem is that you don't even try to quit in the first place. You think to yourself, 'I've really *got* to stop smoking,' and you continue to smoke rather than lose your freedom of choice. You think that once you've quit you'll never be able to smoke again and so you put it off, feeling panicky even at the thought of stopping. So it's a case of: 'I've got to quit, but not today' – and of course it's never 'today'. Even though there are good reasons for you to quit, your sense of freedom is going to be more important than even your health. You smoke to prove to yourself that you're free to smoke: 'See, I have the freedom to smoke. Here I am smoking because nobody can tell me what to do!'

The second problem with all this happens when you do, finally, make an attempt to quit, because that's when you really feel as if your freedom to smoke has been taken away. You've stopped, so you think you can't smoke any more, maybe never again – but certainly not now, because you've quit. Oh dear. You are tied into that cinema seat and maybe you would have enjoyed this film; but all you can think of is how to get away.

If you are trying very hard to stay stopped, you hope these miserable feelings will pass soon: but they don't. In fact they can get worse as time goes on. All the time you are not smoking you are obsessed with it. The one thing you can't have is the one thing you want the most, so you spend hours and hours craving for a cigarette. You feel deprived, sorry for yourself that you can no longer enjoy such a simple pleasure as a good smoke. You feel angry, even filled with rage, and start to take it out on the people around you. Especially those people who pushed you into this depressing situation in the first place. You don't see anything good about not smoking. You've lost your best friends and you are grieving for them. You feel depressed. All the fun has gone out of life and you see little reason to celebrate, socialise or maybe even get out of bed. What's the point if you can't smoke any more? You can eat lovely things to make up for it, but you know where that's going to lead, and you watch with despair as the treats begin to attach themselves to your hips and thighs.

In case you don't already know from bitter experience, these feelings of deprivation are almost impossible to live with for very long. You may try to ignore them, wait them out or try to accept them as inevitable, but as time goes on you begin to realise that the only way to solve this problem will be to smoke again.

Perhaps you hang on until you find a good excuse to smoke, which becomes your final straw. All this misery and then ... this! You miss your train. Your boss yells at you. Your partner lets you down. So you smoke. Not really so much because of the excuse (life is, after all, packed full of excuses to smoke), but because you just didn't want to feel deprived any more. You wanted your freedom back. So you return to, 'See, I have the freedom to smoke. Here I am smoking, because nobody can tell me what to do!'

Except that now you're back smoking, which really, in your

heart, you wish you weren't. Not only that, but now you have another problem. As you go on smoking each day, in the back of your mind you remember what stopping smoking was like. It was miserable. Depressing. The mood swings turned you into a monster. A monster you didn't like very much, and neither did your friends. You gained weight. You felt anxious and found it hard to get anything done. And on top of it all you went back to smoking, so it was a complete waste of time! No wonder you go on smoking for the next decade or so rather than try that one again.

Is it time for some good news? I think so. The truth is that it doesn't need to be like that at all. There is a simple solution and it's extremely effective, provided you're willing to make the mental shift in the way you are thinking about quitting. This solution is for you to think in terms of choosing to stop and choosing to stay stopped. You don't force yourself with 'You have to stop' and 'You've got to stop, or else!' And once you've stopped, you don't threaten yourself with, 'You can't smoke any more,' and 'Don't you dare smoke ever again.'

Instead, you create a completely different attitude towards quitting. You simply understand and remind yourself often that you always have the freedom to smoke. You never lose it. Even if you stop smoking, you still have the freedom to smoke. Even if you end up never smoking again, you still have complete freedom of choice in the matter.

You never *have to* stop smoking. Even if you are ill from smoking, even if it would be a very good idea if you stopped. Even if you desperately want to stop, you still don't *have to*. You always have a choice. You have the choice to continue to smoke and smoke every day for the rest of your life. And even after you've stopped, you still have the freedom to return to smoking at any time. That's a freedom you have just because you are alive and free and walking around in a world where there are cigarettes. It's always your choice whether or not you smoke. And you don't have to do it to prove it.

I'm not encouraging you to go on smoking. It's crucial to be honest about the consequences your choices will bring. If you continue to smoke the chances are that your health will deteriorate. Your self-esteem will suffer. You'll waste money on cigarettes. You'll smell of stale tobacco smoke and so will your house, your clothes and your hair. If you continue to smoke you have a 50-50 chance of dying from it, as much as 20 years earlier than if you had quit. The quality of your life will deteriorate and you will grow older faster. All these things are very possible if you continue to be a smoker, but none of it means you don't have complete freedom of choice about how you live your life. It's your life. It's your body. It's your pack of cigarettes. It's your choice. It's your responsibility.

I'm not encouraging you to smoke the odd cigarette here and there after you've stopped, either. Knowing you have the freedom to smoke makes all the difference, but this means knowing you're free to return to daily smoking any time. Even if you haven't smoked a cigarette for a week or a month, you're still free to smoke. If you do smoke, though, you will return to smoking every day, because smoking is an addiction. You don't have the choice to smoke and not to become re-addicted.

This thing about choice is deceptively simple. So simple, in fact, that some people miss the point. They think it must be much more complicated than this. Or they think that the mood swings and the anguish and the anxiety are caused by their biochemistry going haywire through lack of nicotine. They are convinced that stopping smoking has to be a nightmare. But why suffer any more than you need to? This is the good news: you don't need to feel as bad as that. The mood swings, the irritability, the feeling that all the fun has gone out of life, the sadness and grief, the tension and restlessness, the resentment and feelings of self-pity and deprivation – all of that is completely unnecessary and can be totally eliminated from your experience of quitting.

The only reason anybody experiences these miserable reactions is because they deny their own freedom of choice in the matter: both the freedom to go on smoking and the freedom to return to it any time they've stopped. Mostly they deny their freedom of choice because they are afraid of it. This is why it's so difficult for some smokers to accept that they've still got the freedom to smoke after they've quit. They're afraid that if they give themselves the option of smoking, they will take it and smoke and never stop. So the only way they can contemplate quitting is to think in terms of removing that option, to think in terms of 'I have to quit' and 'I can't smoke any more.' And this is exactly what turns quitting into a nightmare. The more a person denies free choice, the more quitting will be a misery, making it so difficult that they may not even stop smoking at all.

When you overcome your fear of having free choices, when you allow the idea of freedom and choice into your process of quitting, the whole thing turns around and becomes a much more positive experience. When it's a positive experience, it's one you are much more likely to want to keep.

Not only will you want to keep it, but you'll have the control to keep it too. When you remember it's your own free choice to smoke or not to smoke, you put yourself in charge and so you take control. You are calling the shots, you are taking responsibility.

If you deny your free choice, you feel as though you're a victim: 'Poor me, I wish I could smoke but I can't.' This creates the misery of feeling deprived any time you do try to stop, but it also tends to create some form of rebellion.

Rebellion may be the refusal to quit, even though it's obvious to everyone that your life and your health would improve in many ways if you did. Rebellion may be increasing the amount you smoke at even the thought of stopping. And rebellion may be finding excuses – even creating excuses – to return to smoking any time you do quit, perhaps blaming others for the relapse: 'Look what you made me do, you made me smoke!'

It may be very helpful to know that practically everybody has this tendency to evade responsibility and deny freedom of choice. It's very likely that you will think you don't have a choice about smoking. When you do you'll feel deprived and you may want to rebel by smoking. What makes all the difference is whether you fall into those feelings and let them spiral out of control, or correct them when they happen. Correcting them is what the process of stopping smoking is all about. You develop the skill of dealing with these thoughts and feelings, rather than avoiding them altogether.

There's one more thing I want to tell you about choice which may be helpful to you and if it's not, that's OK. You may have seen programmes on TV that show live pictures of brain scans with moving, coloured images of brain activity. This is made possible through some modern technology called a PET scan. It's exciting to be able to see a living brain at work, and research is now being conducted to see what can be learned. There's one experiment I've come across that's relevant to what we've been looking at in this chapter.

Subjects lay in a PET scan doing nothing more than lifting one finger, while the researchers watched to see which parts of the brain were activated during this process. First, they told the subjects which finger to move. Then, they let the subjects decide themselves which finger to move. The difference was clear. As soon as they started to make their own decisions, an area of their brain which had previously been inactive sprang into life. This activity was in the prefrontal cortex, in a region which lies behind the forehead. This is where our ability to choose for ourselves lies.

The action involved in moving a finger was the same in both instances. The difference was in choosing it rather than following orders. In the same way, smokers may go through the motions of quitting smoking, but do it with a frame of mind that says they are just following orders. Could it be they aren't using that crucial area of their brain?

It's now well known in the world of brain research that our brains develop through use, in much the same way as we might strengthen a muscle. Doctors who specialise in brain rehabilitation, after accidents or strokes for example, have found that two things make this happen: *paying attention* to what you're thinking and *repetition*. The more you make choices, deliberately and consciously, the more you activate and strengthen this area of your brain, your prefrontal cortex. It makes all the difference in stopping smoking and this practice in choosing could have an empowering impact on many areas of your life.

WHAT YOU CAN DO

■ *Tell yourself: 'I'm free to smoke'* whenever you think about smoking. While you are still smoking, as you light each cigarette, think: 'I have the freedom to smoke.' It's not that smoking is a good idea, or that it's something you want to continue doing. It's just that it's always something you have complete choice about. If you deny choice you'll feel deprived. When you choose, you can make the choices you really want to make.

■ *Be willing to spend some time* thinking about this before, during and after you quit. It's not that you must never make the mistake of thinking that you 'have to quit' or that you 'can't smoke any more'. Quite the reverse. The chances are you will deny your freedom of choice, at least sometimes. Most people do. What makes all the difference is getting into the habit of noticing these thoughts and correcting them. You correct them by reminding yourself of the truth: that you've got the freedom to smoke, whether you want it or not and whether you actually smoke or not.

What most people do is to consider the consequence of a certain choice, regard the consequence as unacceptable, and so conclude they have no choice! This is so common that almost everybody does it. For example, 'If I go on smoking it will kill me, so I have to quit.' Not true! You could go on smoking and die from it. It's not that this is a good idea: just that it's a choice. The more you get this, the more likely you are to succeed.

■ *Try telling as few people as possible* that you are stopping smoking. If nobody knows you've quit, it may be easier for you to accept that you have a choice about it and that it is yours alone to make.

■ *Do not tolerate the symptoms of deprivation* after you've stopped. Deprivation is a dangerous state to be in, because it can lead you back to smoking. The state of deprivation may show up as one or more of the following: anger, irritability, sadness, depression, grief, loss, self-pity, martyrdom, envy of others, smoking, panic, anxiety, restlessness, persistent and intense desire to smoke, any symptoms of stress, remembering only good things about smoking. Whenever you notice any of these reactions, remind yourself that you have got the freedom to smoke, that nothing has been taken away from you.

As most people feel many of these things anyway, whether or not they are stopping smoking, it's important to see if these feelings or moods have become stronger or more persistent for you since you quit. If so, you are feeling deprived, which is the sign that you haven't grasped a genuine sense of choice.

■ *If you have a hard time believing* you've got choices, this is something you'll need to think about very carefully. You may be caught up in a line of reasoning such as: 'If I smoke I'll ruin my health and I can't possibly do that to myself,' or 'I can't smoke now because I'd feel such a failure.' These may be the consequences of your choice to smoke, but it doesn't mean you don't have a choice. A bad choice is still a choice. You can acknowledge your freedom to smoke and still choose not to smoke. Reminding yourself that you are free to return to smoking later on will help you to make this sense of choice a reality.

- *Grieving over the death of your best friends* is an especially common symptom of deprivation. Most people try to deal with this sense of grief by attempting to convince themselves that cigarettes weren't their friends and that they are better off without them. This is fine, but it probably won't disperse the feeling of grief. Much more to the point is that nothing has died, nothing is gone and lost for ever. This sense of grief comes from thinking that you have made one final choice to never smoke again, a choice to last for your whole life, just as final as death itself. Well, you can't possibly make one choice not to smoke for the rest of your life. All you can do is not smoke for now and hope it stays that way. When you remind yourself that you can always return to smoking, that you can invite these 'friends' back into your life any time, then the sense of finality goes and the grief along with it. It's fine to hope you never smoke again, but understanding that the option of smoking never goes away makes a big difference.

■ *Write down the thoughts* which keep you trapped in your state
   of deprivation. This is the most powerful way to shift your
   thinking, because then you can see these thoughts on paper
   and re-evaluate them more objectively than when they are
   flying around inside your head.

At the top of a piece of paper, write: 'I have to stop smoking
because ...' and complete that sentence in any way you can. For
example, 'I have to stop smoking because my chest hurts.'
Continue to write as many endings as possible. You may be able
to think of seven or eight ways to end the sentence, or even
more than that.

Then, next to each line, write the true statement. For example,
'If I go on smoking my chest will continue to hurt, and I can do
that.' You could use a different coloured pen for the true
statements, so that you can more easily see a contrast between
the two.

The first list of sentences will get you in touch with the
thoughts that create the sense of deprivation for you. The
second list will liberate you from that negative way of thinking.

■ *If you feel deprived after you quit*, it may be helpful to keep
   cigarettes with you. Having cigarettes around may make your
   sense of choice more real to you. Remember, though, to choose
   the consequences as well as the cigarettes. Think in terms of: 'I
   have the freedom to smoke and get ill from it and possibly die
   prematurely. It's my life and it's my choice about how I live.'

Simply accept that you are free to live your life as a smoker.

That you can smoke every day for the rest of your life. That you never have to stop, and even if you do stop you can always go back to it. Then, along with the freedom to smoke comes a genuine freedom not to smoke. When you know you've got choices, then you can make choices.

How I Quit: Tanya

I'm 45, I used to smoke at least 40 a day and I smoked for about 25 years. I quit because I have severe problems with my circulation, and asthma, which I've had all my life. To begin with, for the first week after I stopped, I wanted to smoke so much it was very difficult. I almost caved in many times. What got me through it was saying, 'Maybe I'll have one in a bit ...' I just kept on putting off having that cigarette and I put it off and put it off and so far I still haven't had it. It's much, much easier now, though.

I had never stopped smoking before so I had no idea what to expect. There were good days and bad days. Sometimes I would think about it a lot, but in the end I know I don't want to be a smoker and all that goes with that. It was very difficult for me to see that I had a choice. I kept thinking that if I felt free to smoke I would smoke. So I didn't feel like I had a choice. But telling myself I might have one later stopped me from feeling too deprived, too lost and sad. I always wanted to keep cigarettes with me so I could see I wasn't deprived. I know I could have easily sunk into those feelings and been swallowed up by misery and self-pity, but I kept on thinking if it got that bad, I'd smoke. And I suppose it never did get that bad, because I didn't smoke and now I'm very pleased that I didn't.

Some days I don't even think about it. My breathing is much better and I have more energy. My circulation is better and I began to get the feeling back in my toes and fingers even within the first week after I stopped. My feet are warmer, although still a bit cold in the winter, but I can feel them much more than when I smoked. At first, when my circulation was coming back to life, I could actually feel the blood flowing around, especially in my arms and legs. It was a bit of a creepy feeling, but didn't last long.

I feel a great deal better for having quit. I feel years younger and often people say I look really good without knowing why. I hope I can keep it up now, but I'm a cautious person and I wouldn't want to say I've beaten it. So far so good. Nine weeks not smoking is a miracle to me. Let's hope it stays that way.

One of the best things that has happened is that my dog doesn't smell of smoke any more; she just smells like a dog. Her fur used to stink of stale smoke and a friend of mine had mentioned it to me too, so it wasn't my imagination. My sense of smell has improved a lot, but that isn't always such a good thing. I can smell a smoker a mile off – and I'm ashamed to think I used to smell like that, and my dear little dog too.

CHAPTER 3

RESOLVE THE CONFLICT

Different people make different choices about how they live their lives. Some people live like this. When bills arrive in the mail they throw them away without opening them. If their car starts to make a clunking noise they turn the radio up so they can't hear it. They don't do any housework for ages, and keep the curtains drawn so they can't see the mess.

Whether you live like this or not, one thing is clear: avoiding problems doesn't usually get them solved. Trying to forget about a problem or pretending it isn't there doesn't make it go away. Often it can can make things worse.

Yet when it comes to stopping smoking, this is exactly what most smokers try to do. This is why they don't stay stopped, because the problem hasn't been fixed: it's just been avoided for a while. It may well be that these smokers don't know how to fix this particular problem, so avoiding it or just hoping it goes away is the only strategy they can use.

Well, you don't need to do that any more, because this book is all about how you deal with the problem so that it stays dealt with. At first this way will seem more difficult, because dealing with problems is always more difficult at first than avoiding them. Paying bills costs you time and money and so does getting your car fixed. Doing the housework takes time and effort. In the same way, stopping smoking takes time and effort when you deal with it rather than avoid it. But taking that time and making that effort means you are much more likely to stay stopped in the long term.

So what does it mean to deal directly with this particular problem? Doesn't it mean that you just choose to stop smoking cigarettes? Well, no. And if you've made any attempt to quit in the past, you know it isn't just a matter of not picking up cigarettes and lighting them. There's something else going on that needs to be dealt with. That something else is your memory of smoking, and it's this memory that is the real problem in quitting.

When you think about it, it makes sense. If you can remember one thing you did once many years ago, you are going to remember something you did many times a day, every day, for most of your life. You are going to be reminded of smoking by the things you associated with smoking in the past. For example, if you walk into your kitchen every morning, turn on the kettle for a coffee and light a cigarette, then walking into your kitchen and turning on your kettle will remind you of smoking. If you smoke any time you feel angry, then when you feel angry you will be reminded of smoking and you will want to smoke. If you smoke whenever you have a glass of wine or beer, you'll want to smoke when you have that drink, because it will remind you of smoking.

Usually people try to avoid these situations when they quit smoking, so that they don't feel tempted. People are even advised to do so by various professionals and experts, through books or courses, and indeed this strategy does work for some people, even in the long term. However, if you've tried this before and now you're back smoking, it looks as though it didn't work for you. In fact, it doesn't work for the vast majority of smokers. Most attempts to quit fail, and they fail because the memory of smoking is remarkably persistent. It's been reinforced with every cigarette smoked, maybe 20 or 30 times each day for years and years. That's some memory! So, if your ability to quit relies on your avoiding this memory, you are almost guaranteed to fail.

After you've quit, your memories of smoking are likely to be mixed, both positive and negative. Sometimes you may think of smoking with disgust and wonder why you ever smoked at all. You'll be thrilled that you don't smoke any more and you'll feel revulsion at dirty ashtrays and the smell of stale smoke. Far from being a problem, these sorts of memories will reinforce your motivation to stay stopped. But there will be other memories too, memories of good times, of the enjoyment and satisfaction of smoking. These memories are the ones you need to watch out for, because they are likely to get you to smoke.

These memories will feel like a desire to smoke. Maybe you'll feel your desire to smoke when you finish a meal, especially if there are others at the table who are lighting up cigarettes or cigars. You might have a desire to smoke when you're waiting for the bus or when you get in your car. When you take a break with a cup of tea or coffee. When you're about to start a challenging work project, or when you've just finished one.

At times you'll remember how a cigarette helped you to concentrate or think creatively. You might remember how smoking relaxed you and made you feel more confident at social events. You'll remember how smoking seemed to comfort you when you felt lonely, helped you to cope in times of stress and when it created a bond between you and other smokers.

I wouldn't be surprised if this is the last thing you want to hear, but the truth is that there is no way to remove these memories, these feelings of desire, completely. Like any other memory, they fade in time but they don't totally go away. You've probably heard stories of people returning to smoking months or even years after they quit, so you can see that the attraction to smoking doesn't leave.

This, in a way, is the bad news about quitting, but it's also the good news. The reason it's the good news is because if you know that this desire to smoke is going to happen, then it makes sense that dealing with it is going to work much better than trying to avoid it. When you learn how to deal with the desire to smoke, when you come to accept that it's a normal and inevitable part of life as an ex-smoker, that means you can succeed at quitting, even in the long term.

You see, the main reason you smoke is to satisfy your desire to smoke. It's that simple. You think that having a cigarette would be a good idea and so you light one. You might explain it by telling yourself you smoked because you were with friends who were smoking, or because you felt upset or stressed or bored, or because you wanted to do something with your hands in an awkward moment. The truth, though, is that these circumstances brought on a desire to smoke, which you then satisfied by smoking. Why did these circumstances bring on your desire to smoke? Simply because you smoked in these circumstances in the past. No matter what the circumstances are, all it means is that you are being reminded of smoking. This memory is your desire to smoke, which is the thought or feeling that smoking would be a good thing to do.

Once you realise that this desire is a memory and that you can't stop having memories, then all you need is some way to respond to that memory other than smoking. If you could handle that thought in a different way, then you wouldn't be smoking, would you? Those memories would come and go and if you just noticed them and felt OK about them, then you'd be able to stop and, more importantly, stay stopped.

At first this may well look like a very tall order, but that's what quitting correctly is all about. Part of what makes this possible is knowing that these thoughts of desire do fade in time. And another part of what makes it possible is knowing you are free to satisfy your desire to smoke by smoking – but also that you don't have to.

As we saw in the last chapter, quitting becomes much more troublesome if you make the mistake of believing you can't smoke any more. If you lose sight of the fact that you've got the freedom to smoke, it will seem as if you're losing out on something wonderful and that you've got the bad end of the deal. You'll resent feeling your desire to smoke, you'll want to smoke desperately, and your desire may not fade in time like it should. This is because the one thing you can't have is the one thing you'll want the most. This gets incredibly tough to live with, of course. Which is why it's so important, why it makes all the difference, if you *choose* to stop smoking – and keep choosing to stay stopped. Then you don't feel deprived, so you can actually feel positive towards these feelings of desire. Then you are in charge of the process and you can accept those memories, instead of being engulfed by them.

All you need to do is to train yourself to handle the feelings of desire. This is why quitting this way takes time and effort at first. This is also why quitting this way gives you the greatest chance of long-term success. You will find all the details of how you handle your desire to smoke in Chapter 5.

The feelings of desire will happen a lot at first, especially if you've smoked a great many cigarettes for a great many years. Then during the first week, usually after the first two or three days, they begin to fade, provided you are applying the technique correctly.

The most powerful way to think about it is to freely choose to accept this feeling of desire, because you'd rather do that than spend the rest of your life smoking. Face each desire to smoke as it comes and think of it is a payment you are making. Do you want to stop smoking so that you can have a longer, healthier life, greater self-esteem and a real sense of freedom and accomplishment? You do? Then this is how you get these things: by dealing with these uncomfortable moments of desire. It's a trade-off. If you can regard it as a good trade-off, you are highly likely to succeed at quitting in the long term. Every time you make your choice this way, you take another step towards resolving the conflict which is at the core of quitting.

Quitting smoking is a process of resolving the conflict between two different and opposing attractions or desires. One is wanting to live your life free from smoking. The other side of the conflict is the attraction towards smoking, wanting to smoke, thinking you need to smoke or would enjoy smoking. When you try to quit by avoiding the desire, you avoid resolving the conflict. Then, when the desire returns (and it will!) you smoke. Not because you had a desire to smoke, but because you didn't resolve the conflict for yourself in the first place.

Being in conflict is of course difficult. It's not an attractive prospect, it's not something most people want in their lives. Have you ever seen a cat flicking its tail back and forth? Some people think this means the cat is angry, but Desmond Morris says it's a sign of indecision. The cat is in conflict, needing to choose something: when to pounce for example. It can't decide, so it flicks its tail.

This is a perfect image to describe the conflict so many smokers get caught up in. They are constantly flicking their tails, thinking 'I really must stop smoking ... but I don't want to ... but I should want to because I'm not breathing so well and I cough ... but I really enjoy smoking, I can't imagine not having a cigarette after a wonderful meal or when I'm driving ... but I'll have to quit sooner or later, won't I ... but not today.'

To begin with, smokers do their best to ignore the conflict. They think, 'I'm a happy smoker ... it's not a problem.' Some may keep that up, but most smokers aren't truly at peace with their smoking. And in most cases smoking does become an undeniable problem sooner or later. So one day you get bronchitis, and then you are back with your conflict in your face.

So you stop smoking – but the conflict is still there! 'Oh, I'm really desperate for a cigarette; why did I do such a stupid thing as stop smoking? ... I can't remember ... I'll just have this one ... ' and then you're back smoking again.

After a few rounds of this stopping and starting, never fully resolving the conflict, something else gets mixed into this conversation and that is *failure*. Every attempt to quit that fails builds another brick in the wall of failure at quitting, and after a few more years you come to the conclusion, 'I should stop smoking but I don't think it's possible. I've tried everything and nothing works. I must be a hopeless case.'

If you see yourself here, understand this. You may have tried every way you know to stop smoking by avoiding coming to terms with your desire to smoke. That's why you failed before and there really is no other reason. Now you know differently. Now it's up to you whether you use this new information to stop smoking in an entirely new way, a way which is the opposite of whatever you've tried before. When you use this technique to come to an unconditional acceptance of your desire to smoke, nothing will ever make you smoke. Then, you will be successful at stopping.

You see, it's not a question of whether you want to have a conflict about smoking in your life. You already have it, at least to some degree. Stopping smoking – correctly – is about facing and resolving this conflict, once and for all. You can only do that when you're feeling your desire to smoke, not when you're not feeling it. Here's the section where you can learn how to begin to put it all in place.

WHAT YOU CAN DO

■ *Notice your desire to smoke and name it* by telling yourself, 'I have a desire to smoke.' You'll find it comes in many forms and it will help you to get to know it and what it's like for you. Sometimes it's a thought, such as, 'I'd enjoy a cigarette right now,' or 'Something's missing,' or simply, 'I think I'll have a cigarette.' Sometimes it's a sensation, such as feeling empty, wanting a cigarette in your hands or in your mouth, or a hollow feeling in your stomach which you might think is hunger. If you think you don't know what to do with your hands, that's a desire to smoke.

You probably don't notice your desire to smoke very much while you're smoking. The only time you become aware of it may be when you're prevented from smoking, for example when on a train or in other no-smoking zones. As a smoker, all you are aware of is smoking, and sometimes not too aware of that either. Part of the process of quitting is starting to become aware of your desire to smoke. When you are more aware of it, you can start to take control of it.

■ *You can practise this technique* if you want to, before you stop completely. Practising will give you an experience of all the things I've been talking about, and your own experience will mean so much more to you than anything I can say. I can guide you, show you the way, but only you can take this journey and only you will experience your own particular journey.

It's best to practise for about five days before you stop completely. The way to practise is to get into the habit of noticing your desire to smoke as much as you possibly can. Just go through your days as normal, but start to tell yourself, 'I have a desire to smoke' whenever you think of smoking. In case you have any doubts, here's a sure-fire way to know that you have a desire to smoke: when you're about to light a cigarette.

Once you've noticed your desire, you then remind yourself you have a choice by telling yourself, 'I have the freedom to smoke.' And then you make a choice, either to smoke or to accept that feeling of desire.

If you choose to accept your desire at that time, remind yourself of why you're doing that: because your life will improve in some way as a result of quitting. So you tell yourself something like, 'I choose to accept this desire to smoke because I want to wake up feeling better in the mornings and I want to stop coughing.' That's the trade-off.

Whether you've chosen to smoke or whether you've chosen to accept this desire, you then wait until the next feeling of desire and start the process again. Sometimes you'll be smoking and sometimes you'll be accepting your desire and so not smoking. You might make just a few choices to accept your desire and you might make many; it's up to you how much you do this during the practice session.

You may well find that your desire doesn't go away when you've chosen to accept it. You accept it, and then a few minutes go by and you accept it some more, and then some more again. Then, perhaps, a few minutes later the desire is still there and you decide to smoke. That's OK. You may think that all you did was simply to delay smoking by a few minutes, but that's not the case. What you did, even if it was just for a few minutes, was that you started to get used to feeling your desire to smoke. This is crucial to your long-term success.

If you had delayed smoking by keeping your mind occupied with something else, by keeping busy or avoiding circum-stances where you would normally smoke, then you wouldn't be accomplishing as much. You might be smoking less, but you wouldn't be getting used to accepting your feeling of desire. Remember, that's the name of the game when it comes to staying stopped. That's the purpose of practising. If you practise enough, you may end up smoking less than you normally do, but this is not the main goal.

If you don't want to do this practice, it's OK. You can just jump straight into quitting if you want to. Practising can be helpful because you can learn quite a lot about how it all works, but don't be fooled into thinking that it's the solution to your problem with smoking. At some point, sooner or later, you'll get tired of practising and either return to full-time smoking or move on to quitting entirely.

Five days is a good amount of time for the practice session. It will give you plenty of time to get acquainted with the technique. If you go on practising for much more than that, it's likely to be a case of delaying quitting just to put off that big plunge into the unknown. Then, it's not practising, but using the technique as an excuse to continue smoking, rather than facing the risk of making an attempt to quit. It will always be risky, though, because you will never know for sure how it will turn out. Don't wait for the risk factor to go. It won't.

■ *If you smoke unconsciously* during the practice session, don't worry about it. Lighting up a cigarette without even realising it is very common and is something we'll discuss in Chapter 5. Just wait for the next desire to smoke and work on becoming as aware of it as you can.

■ *If quitting is easy for you* but starting again is just as easy, you are one of those smokers who can easily avoid feeling your desire to smoke for periods of time, probably without even trying. Some people are just like this, while others wouldn't be able to avoid their desire to smoke if you paid them a million pounds.

If you don't have much of a desire to smoke at first, this technique will probably seem unnecessary. However, if you continue to work with it, even though it feels as if you are just going through the motions, then when your desire to smoke does come back, you'll be able to cope with it without smoking. You know your desire does come back at some point, because that's when you've returned to smoking in the past. That's when you really start the process of stopping smoking, and that's when this technique will become invaluable.

It's a bit like learning to swim. You can talk about it and you can read about it, but you aren't going to learn how to do it until you get into the water. In quitting smoking, when you are in the water is when you are feeling your desire to smoke. That's when you really learn the skill of quitting. That's when you resolve the conflict.

■ *Resolve the conflict once and for all* by asking yourself, 'Is it worth it to me to feel this desire to smoke in order to be free from smoking?' Be careful not to dramatise what you feel. The desire is a temporary feeling of discomfort. See if you can locate what it feels like in your body. If you allow yourself to feel that, you get to be free from smoking as a direct result. Then you are no longer in conflict with this feeling of desire, because you are completely willing to feel it.

How I Quit: Mike

When I started smoking I knew it was harmful and would probably kill me, and I went ahead and started smoking anyway. Looking back at that, I think of it as a pact I made with the Devil, and now that I've quit I'm renegotiating that contract. One time, about two days after I stopped, I wrestled with my desire to smoke for 20 minutes. It was as though I was fighting for my life, but it was never like that again. By and large it has been easier than I thought it would be. The desire to smoke comes and goes, and I notice it and I get on with whatever I'm doing. I think of the desire to smoke as the voice of the Devil calling me back.

I used to smoke two or three cigarettes in bed before I even got up. Now I don't even think about it. I certainly think about it at other times but not in the mornings, which I was sure would be the toughest time. I'm waking up an hour earlier than when I smoked and I feel pretty good, clean and fit.

The biggest test was when I got my bike stolen a week after I had stopped. I thought, 'Sod it!' and I thought I would just go ahead and smoke, because what did it matter anyway? I don't know why I didn't have one then. I came very close. I guess I thought I'd be back smoking and my bike would still be stolen. Then I'd be angry about the bike and angry about smoking again. I hated that feeling when I smoked of being so out of control, smoking and then smoking another one and another one. What a waste of time and money. I hate to think how much I've spent over the years.

What I like most now is that I do have the choice to smoke, but I don't have to. I look at people smoking, especially when they are hanging about outside doors or in stairwells, and I don't envy them at all. I just feel a huge sense of relief that I don't have to go and puff away at a cigarette any chance I get, wherever I am.

I used to smoke about 40 a day, so when I see friends they always notice I'm not smoking, because I would have always had a ciggie on the go. I just say I'm trying to cut down and I leave it at that. Most people don't go on about it because they can see I'm not interested in talking about it, so they leave it alone. I like to keep it that way. I think there will come a time when I feel comfortable enough to talk about it with my friends, but for now I want to keep it private. It's a very personal thing, between me and my Devil.

CHAPTER 4

UNDERSTAND ADDICTION

Although you may know full well that you are addicted, I bet you'd find it tough to explain exactly what an addiction is. It helps a lot to understand some things about addiction because then you'll be able to see more clearly what it is you're up against.

First of all:

● *An addiction is pleasurable and satisfying.* The very first cigarette you smoked may have made you feel ill, but there was something interesting about it too, so you tried it again. It may have taken a few cigarettes, but pretty soon you were enjoying it. Even after many years of smoking, there are usually some cigarettes which smokers enjoy or which at the very least provide a sense of satisfaction. People don't usually get addicted to things they find no pleasure in.

The pleasure can fade for some long-term smokers because they become so upset about smoking, feeling so hopeless and guilty about it. But even for those people, there was an element of pleasure that got them hooked in the first place and probably continued for many years. Even if you are now loathing cigarettes, you'll still feel a desire to smoke after you've quit.

Everything in this book works towards helping you to acknowledge and accept the truth that there is something enjoyable about smoking – but at a cost. If you work through this process, you'll be able to weigh it up – the pleasure versus the pain – and decide how you really want to live your life. Eventually you'll be able to see that there is also great pleasure in not smoking, but it's a different kind of pleasure. You weigh up the instant gratification of smoking against the delayed gratification of being free from smoking. Not only is smoking enjoyable, but:

● *An addiction often seems to help.* In case you don't already know, smoking cigarettes gives you a boost of energy, helps you cope, relax and socialise; befriends you when you're alone; helps you to concentrate, to avoid thinking about something unpleasant, make decisions, relieve boredom, deal with stress; calms you down when you're upset, get up in the morning, go to sleep at night, digest your food, satisfy your hunger and talk on the phone; and it keeps your weight down. Although probably not all at the same time. I've no doubt left a lot out, because each smoker has their own personal uses for cigarettes; but you get the general picture. You end up believing that you can't live without cigarettes, or at least can't function very well at all.

Whether or not smoking really does do these things is rather doubtful. Notice that there are a number of contradictions in the above list, which should give you a clue as to how real many of them are. There has been a fair bit of research on all this, and yet very little has been proved as to the genuine contribution tobacco makes to our lives.

Mostly, all that's really happening is that you develop an

association between smoking and certain moments in your life and so, when those certain moments come by, you want to smoke. If you then smoke, you satisfy the desire and reinforce the association one more time. That part of it, though, is usually not completely conscious, so it's easy to believe that smoking helped you through that certain moment.

For example, you need to write a letter. You have associated smoking with writing letters in the past, so thinking about writing the letter makes you want to smoke. You satisfy your desire to smoke by smoking while starting to write. You do this every time you write a letter and end up convinced that you couldn't write a letter without smoking. When in fact all smoking did was satisfy the desire.

You'll be able to see this more clearly after you've quit, especially when you use this technique. This is because you gain the ability to see the desire to smoke as a separate experience. There's writing letters (or whatever), and there's having a desire to smoke; two things entwined, but different.

The way you think about smoking makes up a big part of the picture of addiction, or more simply put:

- *An addiction is in your mind.* This may be tough to hear, but being addicted also means being deluded. The ways in which the addiction tricks and cons you is quite extraordinary.

Perhaps the best and most common example of this is the conviction, after quitting, that smoking one cigarette won't be a problem. Now, if you think about how many cigarettes you've ever smoked, you may come up with a figure in the tens of thousands or even more. In the light of that evidence, the idea that you're just going to smoke one, and that will somehow be enough, is completely absurd. However most people, when they have quit, will seriously consider this as a possibility and a very reasonable one at that. The addictive thinking creates these deceptions, making them appear completely rational.

The con of addictive thinking is usually developed over many years of smoking. For example, whenever you hear about the link between smoking and cancer or heart attacks you may think, 'Well, we've all got to die one day, haven't we?' This defence makes it easier for you to live with yourself while you are smoking; but now that you're quitting it's crucial to start to face up to the truth. Smoking kills. Smoking ages you faster than anything else does. Smoking can make your life miserable by disabling you through a stroke, amputation, blindness or emphysema – none of which is inevitable. The addictive thinking may remind you of that one rare exception, your great-uncle Henry, who smoked every day of his life and lived to be 100 and fit as a fiddle. Or the addictive thinking will make a joke out of it: 'When you quit smoking you don't live any longer; it just seems that way.'

This is why it can help you to keep this book around, so that you can stay in touch with reality in the middle of all the confusion around quitting. Stay in touch with the fact that smoking kills about 120,000 people a year in the UK alone.

Stay in touch with the fact that it's the most common cause of heart disease and cancer. The fantasy of 'It's not going to happen to me' may be the most tragic part of the con.

Addiction isn't just a way of thinking, it's also true that:

- *An addiction involves your body.* If you've ever tried smoking herbal cigarettes, you know how completely boring they are. This is because they don't have that vital ingredient contained in tobacco, the drug nicotine. It's the nicotine in cigarettes that you're addicted to, and smoking tobacco is simply the best way to get it into your body. This is because the nicotine in each puff of smoke is taken straight into your lungs, where it's immediately absorbed into your bloodstream.

The inside of your lungs would cover the size of a tennis court if it was laid out flat (so I've been told). That's an enormous surface area for all those smoke particles to enter your body all at the same time. Whoosh! In a few seconds the nicotine reaches your brain and the 'feel good' brain chemical called dopamine is released. Adrenaline is released into your bloodstream and your heart pounds, giving you a buzzy, stimulated sensation. For a few seconds you feel more alert and energised. You can probably feel this happening when you smoke, maybe not with every cigarette but often enough to keep you interested. Your memory of these countless 'hits' of nicotine is your desire to smoke.

Both mind and body are involved in addiction, so both are involved in breaking free, which is always challenging because:

● *An addiction means you get withdrawal symptoms when you stop.* Most people think of physical symptoms when they think of withdrawal, but there is also a psychological side. It's difficult to completely separate the two, because our minds and bodies are in communication all the time, every moment of our lives. Things that happen in our bodies have an effect on our thoughts and our thoughts affect our bodies.

For example, if you've ever locked yourself out of your house or your car (or done something similar), you can probably remember that sinking feeling in your stomach at the very moment you realised what you'd done. The realisation ('Oh my God, what have I done?') was in your mind. The sinking feeling was in your body.

The desire to smoke works in a similar way. The desire is in your mind and you feel the sensation of it in your body. If you've tried the practising suggested at the end of the last chapter, you'll know what I'm talking about. Whenever you smoke, you alter the biochemistry of your body to give you the 'buzz' and this registers in your mind as satisfaction.

What happens when you quit is that nicotine (which is the active drug in tobacco, the bit you're addicted to) leaves your body in about 24 hours. Your body then begins to recover as much as it can from all the damage smoking has done. This is the physical side of withdrawal, which is a process of detoxification. At its worst it feels as if you're coming down with the flu for a couple of days. In fact, it's the signs of better health on the way. Your runny nose means your sinuses are draining properly. Your cough means your lungs are clearing. Pins and needles in your hands and feet mean your circulation is improving. Feeling lightheaded means there's more oxygen in your blood. The severity of these symptoms will depend a great deal on how much you've smoked and for how long, but they don't last more than a few days and you don't need to do anything about any of it. Just wait it out and very soon things will begin to improve. Then it's all behind you.

The psychological side of withdrawal is different, in that it's something that won't improve unless you get involved in changing the way you are thinking, so that you start to think in more positive and effective ways. This book shows you exactly how to do that, and the more time you spend on it, the better it will work and the more successful you are likely to be.

Unfortunately, some people give up trying before they've even started. One reason for their fatalism can be that they feel doomed from the start because of their genes. It is true that:

- *There are genes for addiction*, and it's very likely that smokers are among those who carry such genes. This could explain why some people are able to smoke now and again, perhaps just at parties, but never get hooked into daily smoking. Perhaps they don't have those genes. In fact, they make up a tiny fraction of all smokers. Most people who try cigarettes get hooked very easily, so if it's the genes they must be very common.

Does this mean that smoking is your destiny? Well, no, because even long-term, hard-core smokers do manage to quit successfully. For example, roughly 44 million Americans have done it. We know their genes didn't change, because genes take many generations to change and this has happened within our lifetime. So don't blame smoking on your genes. Genes simply mean you have the potential to become a smoker. Addiction is something you learn – and you can also learn how to take control of it. Perhaps the most important thing to learn is that:

● *An addiction means you're out of control.* Once the addiction is established, which is probably within the first few weeks of your very first cigarette, it becomes an integrated, automatic behaviour which can never be unlearned. This doesn't mean that you can never quit smoking. What it means is that smoking will always be part of your life experience, even if you don't smoke for years. As you may know, once you've learned to swim or ride a bike, that's a skill you have for keeps. Even if you don't use that skill for years you can recall it any time. If you jump into water you know how to swim. You don't need to learn it all over again.

It's the same with smoking. One cigarette, even one puff, drags you into that familiar, automatic 'skill' of smoking. You learned this skill when you started smoking all those years ago and you never completely forget it.

This is why the choice to smoke is the choice to be addicted, and that means returning to a life of smoking. Day in, day out. That's how smoking is. It's always going to be that way because it's always going to be an addiction.

WHAT YOU CAN DO

■ *Make your choices one moment at a time.* When you acknowledge the reality of addiction you know that once you've quit, if you smoke even one puff you're on your way to returning to daily smoking. You might then assume that you can't have even one lousy puff ever again! This puts you straight into a state of deprivation, because you're thinking you don't have the freedom to smoke, that you've made one choice to quit that will last for ever.

The way out of this is to know that smoking means smoking addictively every day, but also to know that you always have the freedom to do it. Simply make your choices not to smoke last for only one moment at a time. So far, so good. Right now you're not smoking, but who knows? You could choose to return to smoking even after you haven't smoked for a whole hour, a whole day or a whole week. Even after you haven't smoked for a month or a year. You don't know for sure. Maybe you'll end up smoking again and maybe you won't.

Does this sound a bit dodgy? Well, it's helpful to think this way for two reasons. Firstly, it keeps you from feeling deprived. The feelings of deprivation make up everything that is miserable and traumatic about quitting, so it's very good not to feel deprived when you've quit. Secondly, remembering that you can always return to smoking keeps you on your toes, and that can make a crucial difference. Whenever you know there is some real danger, you're likely to be a bit more careful. Knowing you really can end up smoking every day, possibly for the rest of your life, keeps you from risking all for that one crafty drag.

■ *In each moment, choose between all of them or none of them.* Just look at your own experience by estimating how many cigarettes you've ever smoked. You didn't stop at one before, so why would you now?

■ *Notice how you try to justify or excuse smoking.* It's pretty much guaranteed that you'll come up with some unbelievably sensible lines of reasoning as to why you should have a cigarette ... or two ... or three ... Simply notice these justifications and be honest about what they are. This is your addiction talking to you, and it's lying to you again. That's what an addiction does. It cons you.

Don't be in the least bit surprised if you get very creative and think up the most wonderful reasons why you should smoke. These voices will almost certainly come into your head, so don't be fazed by that. Just don't give these thoughts any credibility. Just laugh at them.

■ *Does smoking low-tar cigarettes* help you to justify continuing to smoke? The tobacco industry has marketed 'light', 'mild' and 'low-tar' brands, implying that they aren't as damaging to your health. The unfortunate truth is that these cigarettes don't actually deliver less tar or nicotine and have been found to be every bit as dangerous as the stronger brands.

■ *Break your dependency by facing the desire.* Your best excuses will be attached to circumstances where you smoked in the past. You'll only be able to distance yourself from them by going into these circumstances and facing your desire to smoke head on – for example, the first time you spend an evening in a bar with your friends who smoke. You feel your desire to smoke in this situation and you deal with it, privately. Then the next day, you realise that the evening was fine and that your life is pretty much the same when you don't smoke. Then you can get to see that smoking isn't such an essential part of your life after all. More about this in Chapter 7.

■ *Overcome your fear of failure.* Whenever you worry about quitting, either that you'll fail or that you won't be able to handle some particular situation without smoking, remind yourself that you have no way of knowing what will happen, and be willing to take things as they come.

Taking things as they come is a very helpful adjustment to make when stopping smoking. Some people always want to know what's going to happen and how things will turn out. They fret and worry and imagine all sorts of things. Will I succeed at quitting? How will I get through a party? What will life be like if I don't smoke? Will I be happy not smoking? Will I be able to get any work done?

When you think things like this, bring yourself back to the present time and tell yourself, 'I'll deal with that when I get there.' After all, that really is the only way you can do it, isn't it? Nobody knows for sure what will happen in the future.

It's impossible to smoke in the future; you can only smoke in the present time. In the same way, you can only quit smoking in the present time and hope it adds up to something. It makes a big difference to deal with things as they come, because this takes so much of the pressure and anxiety out of it.

How I Quit: Sally

I joined a health club after I quit smoking, because I thought that if I can keep off smoking then I can afford to do that. I've started going down there right after stopping and it gave me an added incentive. Quite a big added incentive, actually. If I went back to smoking I wouldn't be able to afford to go to the health club, so it would be a double nail in the coffin. I'm really aware that I do have the choice to smoke, though. I know I could smoke and do that again, but it would be an expensive choice. Instead, I'm making an investment in my health.

I need to keep telling myself that if I have one puff, then I'll be back, because that is the real problem for me. That's what did me in last time. I keep thinking it, although I know it's totally illogical. I keep thinking, 'It wouldn't hurt, it wouldn't make a difference if I had one little puff.' It happens most often when I'm with people who are smoking. All my friends smoke and my boyfriend smokes. I think, 'Go on and see what happens when you have one. I bet you can have one and then not have another one until tomorrow.' Then I think that's a trap I don't want to fall into.

I'm 28 and I had smoked since I was 16, about 20 a day. I wanted to stop because I was fed up with it and especially fed up with feeling guilty. Since I quit just over two months ago, my head is clearer in the mornings and I feel much more alert. I'm more alert all during the day too. This has been a surprise to me, because I hadn't known how smoking was affecting me until after I stopped. I feel great, really, with more energy and I feel more positive in general. I think the sense of accomplishment is my strongest motivation to stay stopped.

I almost always get my desire to smoke when I'm with my friends, and it's usually that voice telling me to smoke a few puffs of one of theirs. I keep quiet about that because I don't want to get into a big discussion with them about whether or not I should smoke. Either way, if they encouraged me to smoke or if they told me not to smoke, I don't want them to get involved. It's my decision and I want it to stay that way. If I decide to smoke nothing anyone could say would make any difference.

Sometimes I've had moments of feeling deprived, but it's certainly a lot less of a problem than when I've tried to quit before. Before, I'd get this persistent, empty, gnawing void that went on for days and days and made me feel crazy. It made me feel snappy and have tantrums and feel like screaming.

It's much less of a drama quitting this way. Sometimes I start to think, 'Why do I have to go through all this, when the other people in my life are happily indulging themselves left, right and centre?' It's self-pity, that's what it is. So I think about my choices. I have got the freedom to smoke. When I remember it's my choice it's quite easy to cope with.

I think to myself, 'This is my desire to smoke. I can either satisfy it and go back to smoking or I can just let myself accept it.' It's not hard to accept at all. The hardest part is remembering that it won't be just one puff, it will be another and another and another. When I do remember that, though, I can make that switch into accepting the desire quite easily. Then I'm very sure I don't want to go back to being a smoker every day for the rest of my life. I look at my friends smoking and I think, 'Get a life!!'

I've got through the days since I've stopped and it hasn't been too bad. I'm not a different person. The only difference is that I haven't smoked 20 cigarettes each day and all that goes with that. I'm quite pleased that I'm not dependent on those little packets. It wasn't a good way to live your life, to always make sure you've got some and make sure there's enough before you go out, and how you panic when you run out, looking for shops that are open so you can go and buy them.

CHAPTER 5

HOW TO QUIT

If you want the *very* lazy guide and just to get on with quitting, you've probably skipped the first four chapters and started with this one. That's fine, because I'm going to review what we've covered, tie it all together and put it into a practical plan for you to follow. Just remember there may be details in those chapters that will make a big difference to how it all goes, so read and review them, even after you've stopped.

The most important concept we've covered so far is this: that stopping smoking is all about learning how to deal with your desire to smoke. When you learn how to cope with this desire, how to handle temptation, then you will be successful at quitting. Then, nothing can make you smoke because things will happen in your life that remind you of smoking, so you'll want to smoke, but you'll have a way of dealing with that. You'll be able to remember what your choices are and how to make the choices that keep you from going back to smoking.

Identifying a problem is the first step to solving it, and we've identified this problem not so much as, 'How do I stop smoking?' but as, 'How do I cope with my desire to smoke?' When you are dealing with your desire to smoke in a positive way, then you stop smoking as a result and you can stay stopped long term.

All this may sound sensible and straightforward but, as you may know, there are a few things which can get in the way. If you've tried to stop smoking in the past, you may know that this desire to smoke isn't just an ordinary thought. It can put you into a kind of trance, like a rabbit frozen in headlights. Your addictive thinking gets active and blocks out any other thought from your mind. You forget how good life is when you don't smoke. You forget the risk you take by smoking that first cigarette. You get mesmerised by desire and all you can think about is smoking, as if it's all that ever mattered in the world.

This is why smokers try to avoid temptation when they stop, because temptation is so very compelling. Unfortunately, it's going to happen. That's the bad news. Fortunately, you can train yourself to deal with it. And that's the good news.

In learning how to deal with it, the first step is deceptively simple and extremely powerful. You name it. You tell yourself that you are feeling a desire to smoke and that it's nothing more than a memory from when you were a smoker. What this does is begin to create a little distance from the desire, so that as well as wanting a cigarette, you are also observing yourself wanting a cigarette. This starts to move you out of that trance state, because you are aware of it rather than simply in its grasp.

This is why stopping smoking correctly takes time and effort at first, because you need to train yourself to get used to noticing and naming the feelings of desire, and in doing so begin to step outside them. If you avoid the desire at first, stopping smoking is easy. But then, all of a sudden, you get hit with a desire to smoke and you smoke in an instant, without even thinking about it. And then you think, 'Oh no, I'm back smoking again; how did that happen?' That's the reason many people relapse. Not because they have a desire to smoke, but because they don't train themselves to deal with it.

Naming the desire is just the first step, though, because even though you know full well what it is that's happening, you may still find yourself fighting it. You know it's your desire to smoke, but you hate it and you wish it would go away.

You are likely to fight your feeling of desire because you fear it. The reason you fear it is because you think it will make you smoke. Many people are afraid that their desire to smoke will overwhelm them and make them smoke again despite their best efforts, even though they sincerely don't want to go back to smoking.

There's something very helpful to understand about this which will make all the difference for you. What you need to understand is that this feeling of desire, uncomfortable as it is, doesn't make you smoke. It's wanting to make it go away that would make you smoke. Whenever you smoke the desire is satisfied and it's gone, at least for a while. You feel 'normal' again – but you're smoking. So, by letting yourself feel the desire you gain the ability to quit; you get the chance to break free from smoking. While you feel this desire, you don't smoke as a direct result. Make the desire to smoke your friend instead of your enemy. After all, it's going to save your life. Then, there's nothing to fear.

If you're afraid of the dark, you turn on a light. Shine a light on your desire to smoke and take a good look at it. When you do you'll see there are no monsters there, just an uncomfortable feeling which will pass in time. This fear is the most common obstacle to gaining an acceptance of the desire to smoke. The problem with it is that it makes you fight your desire, and fighting it makes it worse. When you fight it, it fights back. The more you want it to go away, the more it's going to be there.

When you develop a more accepting frame of mind towards your desire to smoke, you will find things get much easier. When you accept it, you relax into the feeling and you simply let your desire be there. Accepting it does not mean you like it or enjoy it. It means you are willing to feel it. It's the opposite of trying to distract yourself, which means you're resisting it. Paying attention to it and accepting it will make quitting go much more smoothly in the early stages, and it will give you by far the best chance of long-term success.

This is simply a matter of saying 'yes' to the feeling of desire. Yes, I'm willing to feel this. Yes, it feels uncomfortable, but I'd rather have this feeling than spend the rest of my life smoking. Yes, it's worth it to me to feel this because it means I'm not smoking. Yes, I'll feel this desire to smoke, because this is the way I get my health back and my self-esteem.

The more you make your choice in this way, the easier it will become and the more natural it will seem.

WHAT YOU CAN DO

■ *Set a date to quit* and write it down so you don't 'forget' it. It's very likely you'll want to put off quitting because it's such a huge risk to be taking. When you stop smoking you take a great leap into the unknown, accompanied by your fears of failure – and probably fears of success as well. Setting a date helps you to get past this resistance and get started on stopping. It will also help you a great deal if you accept the fact that you can never know for sure how it will turn out. Remember, you don't need to know.

■ *The moment you stop smoking* is the moment you raise the stakes. Instead of choosing between accepting your desire or *smoking one cigarette* (which you've been doing if you've been practising), you choose between accepting your desire or *returning to a life of smoking*. The desire can be so intense and persistent at first that it's only when you weigh it up against a lifetime of smoking that it can be chosen as the better option. If you try to choose between accepting the feeling of desire or just smoking one cigarette, the cigarette will win.

■ *Notice your desire to smoke* and make your choice by telling yourself:

I have a desire to smoke
I have the freedom to smoke
Either:
I choose to return to a life of smoking
Or:
For now, I choose to accept this desire to smoke
For the benefits of not smoking
(remind yourself of your own motivation)

■ *Write these words on a card* and keep this with your money or credit cards. Then you can read it if you forget it or parts of it.

■ *Repeat these sentences over and over again.* When you were a smoker, you created a strong memory through countless repetitions, cigarette after cigarette after cigarette. When you stop smoking you need to create a new memory, again through repetition. Repetition is our main tool for learning, whether we are learning to play a musical instrument, drive, swim or whatever. We repeat over and over again, until the new information gets connected up in our brains and the new skill is ours. The skill you're learning here is the skill of dealing with your desire to smoke. Repeat the technique every time you feel your desire to smoke and it will quickly become a natural part of your thinking.

■ *Remind yourself of why you want to quit* by thinking of what you like about not smoking. Make sure they are your own, selfish reasons. It may be the money you save, getting rid of that morning cough, or it may be the sense of freedom, control or accomplishment. Just have it be something for yourself, rather than quitting to please other people. Then it makes sense for you to accept the uncomfortable feeling of desire, because the trade-off is a good one.

■ *If you feel tense or agitated,* try taking a breath and letting tight muscles in your body relax. Let your shoulders drop, your jaw slacken and your hands relax. Just allow yourself to be there with the feeling of desire. In this way you accept the desire to smoke in a physical way as well as mentally.

■ *If you keep cigarettes with you,* you'll be more in touch with your desire to smoke and more able to see that you've got the freedom to smoke. For some people, it makes a huge difference to know that cigarettes are available. For others, it's too much, so choose what's right for you. The main thing is that you know you could get to cigarettes and return to smoking if you chose to do so. This might mean going out to buy some or borrowing some from a smoker, but it's still a choice you always have.

- *If you're in the middle of a conversation* with someone and feel your desire to smoke, finish the conversation and deal with your desire as soon as you can. If you're in a situation where people are constantly talking to you, requiring your attention, it may help you to excuse yourself now and again. Pretend to make a phone call, go off to the toilet or make some other excuse. Collect your thoughts, think through your desire and then return.

- *If you fear you may smoke unconsciously* but want to have cigarettes around you, simply create some kind of barrier between you and the cigarettes, so that you notice what you're doing if you go for a cigarette unconsciously. The barrier could simply be that you keep your matches or lighter in a different place from usual, in a box perhaps. You could tie a rubber band or a piece of tape round the pack of cigarettes. You could stuff a tissue in the cigarette packet or turn the cigarettes upside down.

It's quite common, especially during the first few days, to forget you've quit and just think to yourself that you'd like to have a cigarette. You start to go for your cigarettes, with every intention of taking one and lighting it without thinking, completely forgetting you'd quit and that you haven't smoked at all for quite a while. This may happen, but you'll find that you realise what you're doing at the last moment. Then, you know you've got a desire to smoke and you can deal with it in the usual way. In a worst-case scenario, where you do light a cigarette completely unconsciously, you can take control at the precise moment you become aware of what you're doing.

■ *You might forget what to say* at first, and sometimes you might ignore the desire, distracting yourself by thinking about something else as quickly as you can. Don't worry if this happens sometimes, but in general, the more you deliberately think through these moments of desire, the easier it will become and the more likely you are to stay stopped. Your own internal dialogue – the conscious thoughts you have – is very powerful. You take control back from the addiction, and you take control by the power of the words you say to yourself.

■ *If you're feeling deprived*, it's because you've forgotten that you've got choices, or maybe that you're just paying lip service to the idea without really believing it. If your desire to smoke is very intense and persistent, even after the first few days, this is a sure sign you're feeling deprived, and it's vital you change your way of thinking. Otherwise it will wear you down. You might hold out until a good excuse comes along, but when you feel deprived a return to smoking is much more likely. Chapter 2 will help you to turn this around.

■ *Face the difficulty in the beginning* and then it just gets easier as time goes on. Allow thoughts of smoking to be on your mind, a lot to begin with and then less often as time goes on. For the first two or three days the desire may come in waves. Then, just like any other memory, it begins to fade. But don't pin your hopes of success on its fading. Instead, pin your hopes on your acceptance of the desire, your willingness to feel it. Work towards accepting it unconditionally, no matter how strong it is, how long it lasts or whatever else is going on.

Later on it will happen much less frequently. You might get just one desire to smoke once every few months, each time lasting about one minute. That wouldn't be much of a problem, would it? But if you didn't accept that desire and you smoked instead, you'd be back smoking. This is why quitting this way, by training your mind to deal with the desire, gives you the greatest chance of staying stopped.

How I Quit : Diane

I'm 38 and I work as a financial administrator for a small manufacturing company in south London. I thought I'd give quitting a go partly because of my own concerns about my health and feeling guilty all the time, and partly because my own mother died of cancer, probably brought on from smoking. She was 45 when she died, which is much too young, and this would loom over me as each birthday would come and go and I'd be getting closer and closer to my 40s. So that got me to try stopping, but I didn't really think I would be able to make it. I had no confidence in myself that I'd really stop and it's still completely unbelievable to me that I have done it. I *hadn't ever been grown-up and not smoked cigarettes, because I started when I was 14. It was very strange to me at first, but now I'm used to not smoking and it seems normal to me. It's funny how quickly you adapt to such a different way of life. I used to go through at least 30 a day, so it's a big change.*

The first three days were absolutely awful, and the first week I had a hard time getting to sleep and would wake a lot in the middle of the night. All the time, though, I did feel I was in control and that helped a lot. It was tough but it was OK, because it was all my choice. It was up to me what I did.

I don't say that I'm free to smoke because then I think, 'Well, why not?' I say, 'I'm free to be a smoker and accept the consequences.' That makes me stop and think. Fear of failure was my biggest problem. It took me a while before I trusted myself enough to know I have the choice to smoke and at the same time feel secure that I wouldn't go ahead and do it.

There was a turning point, a scary moment about two weeks after I stopped where I almost lost it. I was with a friend of mine at her house. She smokes and without thinking I had picked up one of her cigarettes as if I was going to smoke it. I was going to go ahead and smoke that cigarette without giving it any thought at all. But something in me shouted out, 'Hey, what are you doing?' and it was like I woke up at that point, as if I had been in a dream. I didn't smoke it, because once I'd realised what was going on, it was easy not to smoke.

I find it easy to accept my desire to smoke, because the benefits of not smoking are quite dramatic. I have a lot more energy and an enthusiasm for life. That might sound funny but it's very strong for me. My circulation has improved, although that took a while to get better, a couple of weeks after I had stopped. And I used to get headaches quite often and I haven't had one since I stopped smoking. That was a bonus for me because I hadn't known that smoking was causing the headaches, but it obviously was.

It's been just over six months now and I get the desire to smoke very occasionally, and it's absolutely no problem for me at all. I don't want to get complacent; I think of myself as quietly confident. Cautious and vigilant. The most helpful thing to me is to think, 'One puff and I'm right back to square one.' Then I can happily choose to accept the desire and usually it goes away then. But it doesn't matter to me if it goes away or not, because I accept it anyway.

I've been through a very stressful three months at work when an audit was going on, and it didn't make any difference to me as far as smoking was concerned. I didn't want to smoke any more than usual, and I wasn't tempted to go back to smoking and use the stress as an excuse. I could have but I thought, 'What's the point?' There are always excuses, even just after you stop smoking; perfect excuses that come right out of the blue, excuses to cave in and have a cigarette. I know I can do that if I want to, but I know it isn't going to get me anywhere except back into smoking.

CHAPTER 6

NO WEIGHT GAIN

There is, of course, a very strong connection between smoking and eating for many smokers. Not for all smokers, though, and it could be that food simply doesn't enter into the picture of quitting smoking for you. If so, you may want to skip this chapter. If, however, you've gained weight in the past when you've quit smoking, or if this is a concern for you now, this could be the most important chapter in the book.

When it comes to this connection between food and cigarettes, different people experience different kinds of problems. A good way to start to understand this is to see where you place yourself, and to do this you answer the 'Desert Island' question.

Imagine you are stranded on a desert island. You will be rescued eventually, but until then you have just enough food on this island to stay alive. There's just a little fruit and some vegetables growing and sometimes you can catch a fish. This is a bit of an unusual island, though, because it also has an unlimited supply of (a) cigarettes or (b) your favourite foods.

The question is whether you'd choose the unlimited supply of cigarettes while you were stranded, or the food – whether it's chocolate, pizza, bread, chips, ice cream, any combination of these or anything else you fancy. And yes, in case you are wondering, there are dry matches with the cigarettes.

Which would you desire the most? You might have a very

clear answer to this or you might be undecided, wanting the cigarettes and the extra food equally. If you get a clear answer, you can see which camp you're in. Either you're a smoker who also happens to eat sometimes; or you are an overeater who smokes – in which case you might smoke for no other reason than that it helps you to control the amount you eat.

● *If you are the kind of smoker who sees cigarettes as more important than food*, then all you need to do is learn to deal directly with your desire to smoke, as explained in this book. The main reason you might eat more after you quit smoking is because you try to satisfy your desire to smoke with food. You get a desire to smoke, which feels as if something's missing, and you try to fill that void by eating. This creates a number of problems.

First of all, the desire to smoke may not be satisfied, because what you really wanted was a cigarette, and the food, no matter what it is, simply isn't a cigarette and so cannot fully satisfy your desire. So you try again with more food, and so on. When you satisfy any addictive desire you reinforce it at the same time. So, by satisfying your desire to smoke with food, you reinforce an addictive desire to overeat. The addictive desire to overeat persists, so the addictive eating persists, along with the inevitable consequence of extra weight.

If you go down this road, very soon, even within a day or two, another problem develops. Your desire to smoke gets hidden underneath all the eating you're doing, so that you're not wanting to smoke very much at all. This makes quitting smoking seem easy. You're not all that interested in smoking – but you're eating everything in sight! Your desire to smoke disappears, maybe for months, and the only problem you can see is that you've put on quite a bit of weight.

This is where things can get really nasty. One day, out of the blue, you suddenly get a desire to smoke, and you smoke. Maybe you never even noticed the desire, and anyway you never did develop the skill of coping with it when you first stopped smoking all those months ago. So now you're back smoking again, but even worse, you've put on all that weight too. So now you're a fat smoker. This happens to so many people who try to stop smoking – but it doesn't have to happen to you. Discover the solutions in the 'What you can do' section at the end of the chapter. First, there's another relationship between smoking and eating to discuss.

There are many smokers who don't eat enough and these smokers have been using cigarettes to satisfy, not an addictive appetite, but a genuine need for food. If this describes you, you are underweight or 'fashionably skinny'. You are a health disaster zone, and the only reason you're not seriously ill yet may be just because you're still young enough to withstand the battering you're giving to your body. This battering is mostly through the excess production of 'free radicals', which are damaged cells in our bodies that create illness and disease. Excess free radicals are neutralised by good nutrition, in particular fruits and vegetables on a daily basis. Your body signals its need for these foods in the form of natural hunger, and you have been overriding that signal by smoking.

When you quit smoking you have the chance to develop a much healthier relationship with food. This means eating when you're genuinely hungry, and this will almost certainly mean you will gain some weight. Aim to eat three pieces of fruit and at least five servings of vegetables each day, and not only will you support your health but your weight gain will be reasonable. In the longer term, your better health, stamina and energy means you'll be more likely to get fitter by taking more exercise and developing a bit more muscle. This will raise your metabolism, so you can quit smoking and look great too.

Let's go back to that Desert Island question. Remember I'm describing very different kinds of smokers here, so see which fits better for you.

● *If you are the kind of smoker who sees the extra food as more important than cigarettes*, it will be better to think about this in a different way. This is to acknowledge that your addiction is really to food. In this case it's very likely that the main reason you smoke is to help you to eat less. With cigarettes, you can take them or leave them, and your problem is not so much about how you can quit smoking: it's about how you can do so and still stay in control of your overeating. The only reason you would ever go back to smoking is that you don't know any other way to stop eating so much. So the only reason you would smoke again is to lose weight, or at the very least not put on any more.

In order for you to quit smoking successfully, you'll need to find another way, other than smoking cigarettes, to take control of your overeating. One thing to know here is that you can't properly take control of your overeating while you are smoking. Smoking covers up the problems you have with addictive eating. So by quitting smoking you have an opportunity to create a new relationship with food, so that you can develop genuine control over what you eat.

It's well known that smoking suppresses the appetite, but many people don't realise that there are two quite different appetites. One is a natural hunger, signalling a normal need for food, and the other is an addictive appetite – in other words, an addictive desire to overeat. Many overeaters rarely feel their natural hunger, because they don't stop eating long enough for it to appear. If this describes you, your smoking most likely satisfies your addictive desire to eat, not your natural hunger. This is especially easy to see at the end of a meal. Clearly you aren't hungry, but without smoking you'll want to eat more and more. This is your addictive appetite in full swing, and smoking a cigarette usually does the trick. After you've quit, it's easy to feed this addictive desire and to continue to eat.

Another link between smoking and eating is to be found in the regulation of blood glucose levels. Our bodies, especially our brains, need a regular supply of glucose in order to work at their best. Glucose enters our bloodstream either slowly and steadily or rapidly, in which case it leaves just as fast. As you might imagine, slow and steady is by far the best for our energy and our health. We get hooked on many things, though, which give us the rapid 'sugar rush' of energy, followed by the sudden crash of depleted glucose in our blood and brain.

Cigarettes create this sugar rush along with most of our favourite snacks: sugar in any form, bread and breakfast cereals being some of the most common culprits. This is part of the reason why cigarettes and addictive foods are so interchangeable; they trigger similar chemical reactions in our bodies.

In order to minimise this connection, aim to eat foods that release glucose slowly and steadily, after you quit smoking. This is especially important if you are prone to these drops in blood glucose and if you normally respond to them by smoking and/or snacking throughout the day. In general, rye bread, jumbo oats and most fruits and vegetables create a sustained glucose release. An Internet word-search for 'glycemic index' will give you more background information and details of which foods to eat to keep your blood glucose levels stable.

WHAT YOU CAN DO

- *If you feel more hunger than usual* after you've quit smoking, find out first of all if it's a natural hunger or an addictive, false hunger. This will depend a great deal on whether you tend to eat addictively in the first place. If you tend to undereat as a smoker, a normal and healthy appetite will be restored and it will be good for you to eat a bit more than you did before.

  If you suspect you're feeling more addictive hunger, be careful not to satisfy this. It can be difficult to tell real from false hunger, so use the following question as much as you can, especially during the first week after you've quit.

■ *Before you eat or drink anything,* ask yourself: 'Would I be doing this if I hadn't stopped smoking?' Then you know if you are about to substitute food for cigarettes and satisfy an addictive desire. Your desire to smoke might appear to you disguised as wanting food, but you can still name it as a desire to smoke and deal with it in the way described in Chapter 5.

If, when you ask yourself this question, you aren't sure how to answer, play it safe and assume it's a substitution for cigarettes. So for example, you feel like eating a bar of chocolate in the middle of the afternoon. You ask yourself, 'Would I be doing this if I hadn't stopped smoking?' If you think, 'No I wouldn't normally eat chocolate in these circumstances,' then you know you've got a desire to smoke disguised as an addictive desire to eat. If you think, 'I'm not sure because sometimes I do eat chocolate at these times and sometimes I don't,' then you play it safe by assuming it's a desire to smoke. You err on the side of caution. The worst thing that can happen is you don't eat something you otherwise might possibly have eaten. The best thing is that you break the connection between smoking and addictive eating.

■ *Break the connection between smoking and overeating* by dealing as much as possible directly with your desire to smoke. Face the difficulty in the beginning and things will get easier as time goes on, even within the first week. The most common mistake is to excuse extra eating by thinking of it as a reward for not smoking. You may justify it by thinking, 'Well, at least I'm not smoking. I can deal with a few extra pounds later on.' Of course you can do that if you want to, but understand that you may be making things much more difficult for yourself in the long run. It's much better to start out as you mean to go on.

There are usually a few tough decisions to begin with, but then it's all downhill from there. On the other hand, when you satisfy your addictive desire with food, you reinforce a stronger addictive hunger next time. It's commonly reported in research that people feel an increased hunger for many months after quitting smoking. What the research doesn't tell you is that these quitters were feeding that hunger, and in doing so they kept it alive. If you don't feed that addictive, false hunger, it fades away fairly quickly within a day or two.

■ *Make all-or-none decisions* about food as much as you can. It can be easy to justify eating 'just a little bit' when you think of it as a one-off choice. You think, 'It's just one piece of toast, after all … what's the harm in that?' Well, it may be one piece of toast, but if it's satisfying an addictive desire it's more likely to be setting up an addictive pattern of eating, which means it's going to continue, probably daily, probably indefinitely. So ask yourself instead if it's really OK with you to be eating this much, in these circumstances, on a regular basis. When you take this whole picture into consideration it may well be easier to accept your addictive desire to eat.

■ *If food is your primary addiction* you will gain more from reading my book on taking control of overeating, also in this series. It's called 'Beating Overeating: The Lazy Person's Guide' and although it's a similar approach to this one, there are a number of details and techniques which relate specifically to breaking an addictive relationship with food.

How I Quit: Jane

I get the urges, especially in the evening, but it's wonderful to have stopped smoking. I never tried to give it up before because I never thought I could. I don't feel deprived at all. Quitting is a gain, not a deprivation to me. And one thing I've noticed is that I haven't eaten as much chocolate as I used to do.

There have been great changes in my life over the last 10 years. I got divorced and two of my three children left home. The third has been seriously ill since she was twenty, although she's doing better now. Smoking didn't help any of the things that have happened. It didn't make any difference at all. There are people who've had terrible lives and they don't smoke. I've never put it in that context before, but I'm able to now.

I have the book here all the time and I keep looking through it. It's my bible. I've written out cards, like postcards. I used cards when I was taking exams for the work I do now. I've made cards and put certain things on them, phrases and ideas that I like. I pick them up and look at them, for quick reference. For example, when I have the desire to smoke, one card says, 'I would rather feel this than smoke,' and that's how I deal with it.

Mostly I have the urge to smoke after I finish a meal. I get home and I'm starving, so I eat my meal and then I get the desire to smoke.

It isn't painful. It's absolutely wonderful that I've stopped smoking. The uncomfortable feeling of desire is minor. The desire to smoke in the morning, which I thought would be terrible, I don't even get that one any more. Which is really odd, because I used to think I wasn't human until I'd had a couple of cups of coffee and a cigarette.

I might get the desire a couple of times in the evening and in the middle of the night. When I get up in the early hours and make a cup of tea, I get it then. That was when I would have had a cigarette, of course. I would smoke one and then go back to bed. But the strongest desire is after my evening meal.

I do realise that I'm only a puff away from disaster. I caught a whiff of someone's cigarette when I was out last night, and I thought, 'That smells wonderful.' It would be easy to pick up a cigarette and take a puff, but I know that would be it and I'd be stuck with smoking again. What a disappointment that would be!

CHAPTER 7

HELP IS AT HAND

'There are more ways to kill a cat than choking it with cream,' as the old saying goes. Well, there are a great many more ways to quit smoking than anybody could or would want to put in a book. I once met a man who told me that the way he stopped smoking was to keep his hands in his pockets. I couldn't argue with him. He had quit for almost 20 years, so there was no doubt it had worked for him.

You may have heard other ex-smokers' success stories. They locked their cigarettes in a box, they only smoked on the hour, they only smoked one out of each pack of 20 and threw the rest away, they made bets with friends; and, of course, they went to see hypnotists and acupuncturists and bought packets and packets of nicotine gum. There could be as many ways to stop smoking as there are people who have done it.

Whatever method you choose to help you, one big plus will be that it helps you to get started. Beginning the process of quitting is the first crucial step, and joining a local group, getting hold of some nicotine patches or making arrangements with the friend who is going to support you can be that first step. After that, though, you'll want to know if the method you choose will help you or hinder you.

Many methods, including those in most self-help books, aim to help you to deny or avoid feeling your desire to smoke.

Inasmuch as this actually happens, that's how successful these methods are. They succeed long term if you are one of those smokers who can stop and never feel tempted again. Some people have quit successfully that way. However, if you've already tried this and avoidance hasn't worked for you, then learning how to cope with your desire to smoke is your only alternative. For the vast majority, this really is the only way to stay stopped in the long term.

This doesn't mean, though, that some other methods won't help you at all. Just be aware that if stopping is a bit easy, you're probably not feeling your desire to smoke very much. Maybe this will last in the long term, but the odds are it won't. It might be better to face that desire from the beginning, so you learn to deal with it directly while the process of quitting is at the forefront of your mind. Then, the fundamental conflict gets sorted out and you can proceed with confidence, in the knowledge that nothing worse can happen and that nothing can ever make you smoke. You feel your desire to smoke, which in time becomes much less intense and much less frequent. You deal with it when it's there and you get on with your life. This is the most powerful way to take and stay in control.

Having said that, it may be that this seems a very tall order for you, and some help at the start will make a big difference. It partly depends on how much you've smoked and for how long. If you've only smoked a little for just a few years, there will be less of a desire to smoke ingrained in your memory. So, especially if you're a lifelong smoker, you may want to enlist the aid of Nicotine Replacement Therapy and/or Zyban.

Nicotine Replacement Therapy

Nicotine Replacement Therapy (NRT) is available in many different forms. The theory behind it is to give you a way to get nicotine into your body without smoking, so that the physical withdrawal is less intense. While you take the NRT (whether it's as a patch, chewing gum, inhalator, micro tabs, nasal spray or lozenge), you get used to living your life without smoking cigarettes and at the same time you gradually wean your body off its need for the drug. The idea is to use weaker and weaker doses of whichever product you are using, so that eventually you stop taking nicotine altogether, with minimum withdrawal symptoms.

The patch allows nicotine to be absorbed into your bloodstream through the skin, and the spray through the lining of the nose. Nicotine is absorbed through the inside of your cheek when you use the gum, the inhalator (which is shaped and used like a cigarette) the micro tabs or the lozenges. The trick with the gum is to chew it just a bit every now and then to release nicotine, and then to rest it between your gum and cheek. If you chew it continuously like ordinary gum you release too much nicotine all at once. If you don't like chewing or if you wear dentures, you may prefer the micro tabs or lozenges which are designed to dissolve slowly in your mouth.

Some people use combinations of these, say patches and gum, at the same time. It's virtually impossible to overdose on NRT because if you take too much you start to feel dreadful: nauseous, dizzy and sweaty. You would know immediately if you had taken too much and it would be a struggle to continue to do that. Most people find their own preferred form of NRT and the right dose for them through trial and error.

Many people say that NRT takes the edge off the difficulty of quitting but that some desire to smoke remains. The desire remains partly because you have far less nicotine in your blood than when you smoked (as much as five times less), but mostly because the nicotine isn't delivered as quickly as when you smoke, so isn't as satisfying. So by all means use the NRT if you want to, but you will greatly improve your chances of success by combining it with building a positive, accepting frame of mind towards your desire to smoke.

One extra problem with NRT is that some people get hooked on it, especially the gum and spray. They continue to satisfy and reinforce their desire to smoke, and so they keep their addiction alive and never make that jump into quitting entirely. Nicotine in any form is bad for the heart and has now been linked to cancer as well, so it's not an ideal solution in the long term. NRT is still much healthier than smoking, but is intended for use as a short-term aid during the first few weeks or months after quitting.

Bupropion

Bupropion (trade name Zyban) is the antidepressant used to help smokers quit. It was discovered almost by accident when some smokers who were being treated for depression stopped smoking without even trying. Zyban has been given a great deal of publicity and is often thought of as a 'magic pill' success story.

In reality, it's a helpful aid for some people, but long-term success is much more modest than its reputation may lead you to believe. A few studies have been carried out which compare groups of smokers taking either Zyban or a placebo, dummy pill.

Zyban does improve the success rates but not by a huge amount, maybe by 10 or 20 per cent. So it's worth using – but don't expect it to do all the work for you.

There hasn't been a great deal of research done on Zyban, probably because it's been so popular. Research is extremely expensive, and most of it is paid for by the pharmaceutical companies who invest in research so that their products can become credible in the marketplace. Zyban has sold so well, though, that it hasn't needed to be proved.

The studies that have been done so far have produced rather contradictory results, so in terms of how it works and how well it works, more questions have been raised than answered. In some studies, Zyban made the desire to smoke much less, but in other studies it didn't. Some people studied didn't feel so depressed after quitting, but for others Zyban brought no improvement at all. One finding that has been consistent is that Zyban helps keep weight down after quitting, especially while you are still taking it.

There are some side effects, too, although not everyone gets them. Most common are insomnia, dry mouth, nervousness and headaches. A few people have allergic reactions and nausea, and there may be a slight increase in the chance of having fits (seizures), although this is quite rare. If you get any side effects it may help to reduce the dose you are taking.

Available only through prescription from your doctor, it would not be prescribed to you if you are already taking an anti-depressant; if you are pregnant, breast-feeding, or under 18; or if you have (or had) an eating disorder such as anorexia or bulimia; or if you have a personal or family history of fits, blackouts or seizures. Zyban could be dangerous when combined with a more than modest alcohol intake. Your doctor is the person who will be able to assess whether or not it's advisable for you to try Zyban.

The way it's used is to start to take the course of treatment for a week or two before you plan to quit; then to continue to use it for another six or seven weeks after you've stopped smoking. Be especially careful when you end the course of treatment, because it's then that your desire to smoke and/or eat may resurface.

Perhaps one way to describe it is that Zyban may put part of the withdrawal process 'on hold' for a while. This isn't necessarily a bad thing. It can give you a great deal of confidence after not smoking for a couple of months, get you accustomed to life without cigarettes and give you a good experience of the benefits of not smoking, such as better breathing and more energy. Just remember that another phase of withdrawal may present itself when you stop taking it. This doesn't have to be a problem if you return to this book and start (or restart) to cope with your feelings of desire. It may seem that things are getting more difficult, but in time this difficulty will fade as you work through it.

The way you work through it is to allow yourself to face the conflict of wanting to smoke while at the same time wanting to remain smoke-free. This, fundamentally, is the process of stopping smoking and it's an essential part of quitting for almost all smokers. If the pharmacological methods – NRT and Zyban – took away all desire to smoke, completely and permanently, they would be 100 per cent successful. They are a very long way from that, so improve your chances of long-term success by learning to cope with your feelings of temptation when they happen.

It may be helpful to understand why this desire continues – and especially why it's so important to let yourself experience it. In the past, you may have been told that you feel a desire to smoke because levels of nicotine in your blood have fallen, either after you've quit or just because you haven't smoked for a while. This is the principle behind NRT, which replaces at least some of the nicotine in the bloodstream. However, when it's pointed out to them, most smokers can easily see that their desire to smoke comes from their memory. You may feel the desire in your body because mind and body are powerfully connected, but the desire clearly comes from your mind.

For example, even after you've quit for a week or more, if you get some disappointing news, you're likely to want to smoke. It doesn't make any sense at all that the levels of nicotine just happened to drop at that moment. What makes sense is that you built an association between smoking and feeling upset, so when you feel upset you think of smoking. It's an inevitable memory of the smoking you did in the past.

Let's look a little closer at how memories get created in your brain. As you may know, each cell in your brain communicates with other cells by sending signals. A single cell pulses a signal to the next one, which pulses to the next one and so on. There are billions of cells in our brains, so the directions in which these pulses could go are almost infinite. The signals don't travel at random, though. They establish familiar routes, patterns which form your particular ways of thinking, everything you remember.

These patterns are created by brain cells which team up, linking themselves together chemically, so that when one of them sends off a signal the other one does too, automatically. This means you get to remember something. All of your memories and your knowledge are formed by these linked connections between the cells.

The more you repeat any thought or action, the more these same cells get activated in the same pattern and the stronger their connection becomes. For example, if you smoke whenever you feel bored, this means the brain cells for 'I'm feeling bored' have become linked to the brain cells for 'Have a cigarette.' Of course, most smokers thoroughly integrate smoking into their lives, so it isn't just feeling bored that triggers the 'Have a cigarette' memory. The cells for 'Have a cup of coffee' are also connected to 'Have a cigarette'; and 'Answer the phone'; and 'I feel angry.' And so on. And so on.

The really interesting part is how all this changes when you stop smoking. You see, when a particular pattern is no longer reinforced, the cells begin to disconnect. Starved of stimulation, the partnership between the cells begins to break down. The crucial point is that the cells that formed one side of the partnership need to be pulsing their signals in order for this to happen.

In our first example, you need to feel bored and then not smoke in order to break that particular connection. The connection doesn't disappear instantly of course, so the first time you feel bored after you've quit, you feel a strong desire to smoke. If you then let yourself feel that, without reinforcing the smoking or creating any other associations, the connection starts to weaken. You don't achieve this when you quit smoking by avoiding boredom, by keeping yourself busy and your mind occupied with other things. At some point, as soon as you do feel bored, you'll want to smoke.

Disconnecting these cell partnerships isn't really as difficult as it may sound. We do it all the time anyway; memories are formed as we learn things and lost when we forget them. We all know that memories fade, so we know that the connections change all the time. However, the linked cells often don't disappear completely. Traces of the old connections remain, which is why some desire to smoke is always likely to occur. This is why the desire needs to be accepted and why you need to develop the skill of handling it when it's there. Not only does some desire continue, but it's much easier to re-establish the old cell partnerships, which is why it's so easy to fall back into regular smoking once you've taken that first puff.

This explanation of brain function is simplified, of course, but is essentially how it works. We know we learn and remember things by repeating them over and over, whether it's a new telephone number, a foreign language or any other skill. We also know that certain memories (our 7 times table, for example?) can be forgotten when we don't practise and reinforce them regularly.

As for quitting smoking, we can see from this why it may not be so helpful to avoid circumstances in which you used to smoke. It also explains why you are likely to get a strong desire to smoke the first time you encounter one of these circumstances, no matter how long it is since you last smoked. As an example, I met a woman recently who told me she had completely stopped drinking alcohol when she quit smoking. After not smoking or drinking for a whole year she went into a pub and ordered a drink. She told me that her desire for a cigarette was as intense as the first week she quit. The good part about it is that she didn't smoke, and afterwards found drinking alcohol much less of a problem. I would have advised her, though, to get that one over with much sooner.

If you keep facing the difficulty at the beginning, it's all downhill from there. Every time you let yourself feel your desire and you don't smoke, you weaken the connections, which is why the desire fades. But remember, things will happen that you automatically connect with smoking, and the first time they occur, the connection will be strong and you'll feel a strong desire to smoke. You haven't necessarily been avoiding them. They may not happen all that often: examples are memories connected to holidays, or visiting certain places, or certain feelings.

It's so very helpful to understand this, because a great many otherwise successful quitters return to smoking when they get caught out by these situations. It's not the initial tough couple of weeks of quitting that trips them up. It's the occasional but quite strong desire to smoke that comes out of the blue, perhaps the first time they feel lonely or the first time they're under a lot of stress. Or the first time they are tanning themselves on a beach, or the first time they are celebrating something wonderful. They return to smoking and say, 'I smoked because I was stressed' (or on holiday or whatever). Now you can see that they smoked because they had a desire to smoke, which they satisfied. Their desire was simply brought on by a memory, a connection they hadn't experienced since they quit.

WHAT YOU CAN DO

■ *Improve on your chances of success.* Ads for NRT are very fond of telling you that using it doubles your chances of success.

What they don't tell you is that this is based on research results of about 4 or 5 per cent doubled to 8 or 10 per cent. In other words, out of every 100 smokers trying to quit on their own, 4 or 5 manage to quit completely for at least one year. If those same 100 smokers had used some form of NRT, maybe 10 of them would have made it. If they all joined a support group, the figures without the aid of NRT would be about 10 per cent and for those using NRT about 20 per cent. This isn't bad, but there's lots of room for improvement, don't you think? That room for improvement is to be found in facing and learning to accept and manage your desire to smoke. Then, the sky's the limit. It's simply up to you – and this book!

■ *Keep to all your routines*, facing all those situations where you used to smoke. When you've quit smoking before you may have reasoned, 'I always smoke every time I go to a party' (or spend time with smokers, or drink wine, or spend an evening on my own, or whatever). 'So I won't do that, and this will help me to stop smoking.'

Now you know better. Now you know that as soon as you find yourself in that tricky situation (and of course you will sooner or later) you'll feel your desire to smoke. When you try to avoid the tricky situations, you are trying to avoid temptation. But it is this very temptation, your desire to smoke, that is the process of stopping smoking. It's only when you feel tempted that you can resolve the conflict which is at the heart of quitting. When you've resolved this conflict, that's when you are accepting your feelings of desire. Then you are able to quit smoking successfully. This means you go through your life, you feel tempted to smoke at times and you don't smoke, because you have mastered the art of dealing with those temptations. The tricky situations will no doubt be challenging, but see them as opportunities rather than catastrophes.

■ *If you want to change some routines*, for example, to sit in no-smoking areas or stop going into the smoking room at the office, just wait a week or so after quitting. Aim to face these circumstances at least once or twice and then you know you're not trying to avoid them. Then you know you have nothing to fear.

■ *Work towards accepting your desire unconditionally.* Be careful not to put conditions on accepting your feeling of desire, such as, 'I'll accept my desire to smoke if I'm calm but not if I'm upset.' At some point you'll get upset and you'll want to smoke. If you made your acceptance conditional in the first place, you're much more likely to smoke.

■ *The desire connected to emotions* can be tough to handle, because you're feeling the emotion – maybe anger, sadness or fear – while you're dealing with your desire; for example, if you used to smoke whenever you felt angry with your children. You'll find it is possible to calm down without smoking, especially if you are clear about accepting your desire to smoke. It may help to take yourself away and sit down and think for a few moments, but once you've done this a couple of times it will become a lot easier. I wouldn't be surprised if you've felt angry with your children while in a no-smoking area, such as a shop. How did you handle your anger then? I expect you smoked a cigarette as soon as you could, but you can see it is possible to handle the anger and the children without smoking.

Provided you've not created that mental state of deprivation, emotions don't become all that exaggerated after quitting. This is because nicotine doesn't alter your state of consciousness all that much. The same is true for feeling stressed, which is also exaggerated by denying free choice when you've quit. Smoking is a serious cause of stress, not a relief. It only seems to relieve stress if you're telling yourself you can't smoke. This is why it's important to know you're freely choosing to accept your desire.

■ *When considering other techniques to help you stop*, always ask for the long-term success rate of that technique. One year is a good amount of time by which to measure results. So if you go to a hypnotist or acupuncturist, ask them what percentage of people they treat for smoking are still not smoking one year later. Many practitioners make claims of success such as: '80 per cent of smokers stop with this technique.' But the real question is: 'How many stay stopped?' If the technique helped them to avoid their feelings of desire, stopping is easy and the success rate will be high; but as soon as the desire returns, returning to smoking is even easier. They help you to stop, but don't help you to stop yourself from starting again.

How I Quit: Claire

Today I saw someone smoking, and it made me realise that there are huge chunks of time when I don't really think about smoking at all. It's surprising to me, considering how many years I smoked, that it can be like that. After 16 years of smoking and just ten days of not smoking the associations, the thoughts about smoking, are going away. I suppose today they've only been there five or six times, and considering I smoked at least 25 a day, that's amazing to me. Sometimes it's a quick thought, in and out of my head in a second, and sometimes it's really there, like a yearning in my stomach. I think, 'God, I'd really like a cigarette.' Even then, though, it's gone fairly quickly.

I'm very aware of my choices. I'm very aware that I could have a cigarette now if I wanted to. I saw someone walking out of a newsagent's shop with a brand new pack of cigarettes and they were taking the wrapper off. I thought, 'I used to do that. I used to really enjoy that, walking out with a brand new pack and taking off the wrapper.' I thought, 'How sad, that was really so lovely.' But then I thought: 'You can do that, you know. You could buy a pack and just take the wrapper off. And anyway, you can go back and be a smoker again if you want to.' There's no reason to feel sad, because I can have it any time I want.

I've come unstuck with quitting smoking attempts in the past because I have tried to do it for other people, especially for a close friend of mine. It got into an absolutely ridiculous thing, where she would snatch the cigarettes away from me and say, 'What are you doing?' and I got locked into this terrible anger and total rebellion in the end. Then as soon as I went on holiday, as soon as I was out of sight, so to speak, I smoked. It didn't work for me, so doing it for myself makes a lot of sense. It's difficult not to talk about it to my daughter, though, because she wants to know, she wants me to quit. But now I don't feel locked into any obligation to anybody. It gives me a sense of freedom.

I was reading in the paper the other day about the actors who were in the old cigarette ads. One woman who advertised Lucky Strikes had her voice box removed and part of one lung. She had smoked for 30 years and she had all that go wrong with her. And the Marlborough Man died from lung cancer through smoking. It really brought it home to me and a huge sense of relief came over me. I thought how lucky I am to be out of it all. It's the first time I've ever been able to read a real scare article about smoking, and I thought, 'Great, this doesn't affect me any more.' I like that feeling very much.

CHAPTER 8

YOUR SUCCESS STORY

Make no mistake about it, tobacco is one of the most addictive substances on the planet, if not the most addictive of all. Many people think that 'hard' drugs such as heroin are far more addictive, but there's a much bigger proportion of people who try heroin a few times but don't get hooked on it, than people who only ever smoke a few cigarettes. Very, very few people try smoking cigarettes and then lose their interest and don't become regular smokers.

Heroin seems more dangerous and of course in many ways it is, because when people do get hooked their lives and their health get wrecked so dramatically. Tobacco is more subtle, destroying your health so slowly that the smoking lifestyle is well established before you become aware of any damage it's causing.

This is partly why it's so easy to get hooked on cigarettes, and why so many people continue to smoke, even today when we all know about the health risks. Smoking doesn't ruin your friendships, make it difficult to bring up children or get in the way of earning a living. Well, maybe just a bit for some people, but most smokers find compromises such as smoking outside, so they can go about living their lives in a very normal way. Smoking tobacco doesn't make you drunk or high. Cigarettes are legal and very easy to obtain. Smoking is not so expensive that you need to embark on a life of crime to support your habit. Well, not yet anyway, for most people. And it's relatively socially acceptable, even now, especially in some social groups.

This is partly why quitting smoking can be such a challenge. Not only do cigarettes become a normal part of your everyday life, but they are an everyday part of the lives of many of those people around you. You probably have friends or family who smoke, and even if you don't, you'll see others smoking on the street, in bars and restaurants, in films and on TV.

After quitting, you will need to be vigilant. Not every single moment of the day, but there will be moments when your desire to smoke returns and it's likely people around you will be smoking, making it look like an obvious, sensible and completely innocent option. These can be your strongest moments of temptation and these moments may never completely go away.

They will happen much less often, though. This means you can go through fairly long periods of time when you feel confident you've kicked it for good – but just a while later on find yourself on the brink of smoking. Be wary of complacent over-confidence. More than anything else, your motivation to stay stopped will make the crucial difference. If you deliberately recall what the consequences of your choices are, you will be able to continue to make the choices you really do want to live with. This is why it's so important to be very clear about your motivation to quit at the start – and to remember exactly what it is you like about not smoking.

One of the best reasons to stay stopped could be that you are no longer contributing to the tobacco industry, which is possibly one of the most deceitful and unethical industries ever. You might think that the tobacco executives would own up to being involved in a bit of a nightmare, admit defeat and retire gracefully. No way. They dedicate their lives to keeping as many people hooked as possible, especially the young, because there's a good chance they'll have a customer for life, albeit a short one. Their customers either quit or die in huge numbers every day, so they use any means they can to keep people smoking and to get youngsters to start. It's called 'marketing'.

As controls on advertising have come into place, the industry and its agencies have fought back and came up with 'brand stretching', which promotes the brand names of cigarettes through other products, such as Camel Boots and Marlboro clothes shops. For as long as it's legal they'll use sponsorship, especially of sports of course, to bring themselves credibility and to connect their brands to exciting and glamourous events. Sponsoring a Formula 1 car demonstrates to all that a brand is wealthy and successful, in other words, a 'club' worth joining. Sponsoring a university gives out an even more prestigious message.

Young people are particularly easily influenced, as the marketing people know well. For example, it could hardly be a coincidence that Benson & Hedges is the most popular brand with children in the UK, and also the most heavily advertised. Advertising agencies have been advised, 'When targeting youngsters, advertisers should present the cigarette as one of the few initiations into the adult world and as part of the illicit pleasure category of products.' This is from leaked internal industry documents.

A survey of popular Hollywood films over the last ten years showed that if you are a character in a film, you are eight times more likely to smoke than if you are a real person. Characters smoke in films so much that it seems normal and, of course, 'cool.' That's why the tobacco companies pay so much money to have the heroes smoking; it's a deliberate tactic to target the young. Film producers regularly accept funding from tobacco companies in return for 'product placement' on screen. For example, Sylvester Stallone accepted $500,000 in return for smoking in the Rocky and Rambo films. How could it be possible that vast numbers of children all over the world are not influenced by this?

A great deal of money is at stake, of course. The manufacturers of Marlboro cigarettes, Philip Morris, announced their earnings rose from $1.81 billion to $1.95 billion in the year 2000. The rise is largely due to overseas operations.

Smoking around the world has actually increased over the past couple of decades, as a direct result of an aggressive drive to market cigarettes in less-developed countries. For example, over 70 per cent of Chinese men now smoke, compared to about 30 per cent currently in the UK. Less-developed countries are perfect targets for marketing strategies that have been made illegal in Europe and the US. Often there are no health warnings on cigarette packets and no restrictions on advertising, even on television.

In many cases the smokers in these countries aren't fully aware of the health dangers of smoking. Unfortunately this is beginning to change, as these countries are now becoming familiar with what they call the 'diseases of affluence'. Tobacco is the major contributor to them all: chronic heart disease, diabetes, osteoporosis, emphysema and high blood pressure. Worldwide, smoking causes more cancer than all the other causes of cancer put together. The World Health Organisation reports that smoking is now the most common cause of death in many of the Third World countries.

Third World smokers are often eager for the status that American or European cigarette brands give them and to exploit this, white, Western models are used in the advertising. The big money of Western tobacco companies contributes 'generously' to aid community programmes and local health schemes, such as vaccination programmes. Teenagers are targeted through sponsorship of night clubs and popular music. Free cigarettes are distributed and the cigarette brand name, logo and colours are prominently displayed so that adults and children alike are aware of who their 'benefactors' are.

If all this doesn't reinforce your intention to quit, be aware of how those in the tobacco industry regard you. More and more tobacco industry employees are leaving their jobs, disgusted with the ethics of their industry. When they leave they often take secret documents with them, handing them over to the press. These leaked internal communications show how cynical the industry is, with nothing but contempt for their customers. One memo describes smokers as 'pretty down-market', saying that 'Anything too clever will go over their heads'. Another describes them as 'slobs' and another as 'insecure and inarticulate'. Ethical qualms or moral considerations about continuing to promote tobacco are never acknowledged.

Tobacco industry strategies are well financed and insidious. They rarely leave any stones unturned. Their agents regularly seek to undermine public health policies (usually with familiar cries for 'freedom of individual rights') and discredit government ministers.

They are heavily implicated in the worldwide smuggling trade, currently being investigated on both sides of the Atlantic. They even hired scientists to infiltrate the World Health Organisation, misrepresenting research and attempting to influence top-level policy making.

Things are changing, though, to counteract this marketing and promotion, and the rate of these changes is gaining momentum. California led the way, with the very first smoking bans in public places and a huge public health programme. It now has the lowest proportion of smokers at 17 per cent, and the incidence of lung cancer, bronchial cancer and heart disease has dropped dramatically as a result. This result has echoed loudly around the world. For example, the government in India has now banned tobacco advertising, sponsorship of sports and cultural events, and smoking in public places.

Legislation such as this supports the fight against the tobacco companies' callous greed. But little is gained unless smokers themselves face their fears and take their own steps toward quitting for good.

You can now begin to accept the truth about smoking. Stop pretending smoking is cool. It's more than merely a bit smelly or expensive or inconvenient in no-smoking zones. It's deadly. It's addictive. It's a cultural con which profits a few at the expense of the health of millions. Learn to see the difference between your addictive desire and your true intentions – and you can take control and quit smoking.

WHAT YOU CAN DO

■ *When did you last feel* your desire to smoke and how did you deal with it? It's usually a great relief when your desire to smoke begins to fade, but deal with it when it's there and you are much more likely to stay stopped in the long term.

The desire to smoke is usually intense when you've just quit and you may struggle with it quite a bit. This is you wrestling with the conflict. Later on it becomes more like a thought. Then, it's easy to dismiss, to think of those stronger feelings as the desire but the lesser, faded memory as nothing at all. Smoking may simply 'cross your mind' very briefly. Well, that's still a desire to smoke and it's wise to keep in the habit of dealing with it as much as possible. Remind yourself of your choices, and (assuming this is the choice you want to make) deliberately choose to accept the desire as a trade-off for some particular benefits you receive.

■ *What do you like about not smoking?* At first you might be completely enthusiastic about quitting, feeling so much healthier and thrilled with your accomplishment. It's not unusual, though, for this high to wear off after a week or so. Then you can run into a dry patch, when quitting has lost that magic novelty value. It can seem like years have gone by since you quit, and you tend to forget what it was like to be a smoker.

This is especially the time to pay careful attention to what you like about not smoking, to make a deliberate effort to remember how your life has improved. Remember that this is the trade-off for accepting your desire and, if there isn't a good trade-off or if you've forgotten what it is, satisfying your desire is much more compelling.

One way to reconnect with your motivation is to consider the option of returning to being a smoker. Think to yourself, 'I can return to smoking and smoke every day for the rest of my life.' Consider that option carefully, and your motivation to remain smoke-free should stand out very clearly.

- *Keep choosing* by reminding yourself that you haven't made one choice to last for the rest of your life. Once you've quit for a few weeks it's easy to fall into thinking that you've kicked it for good, so counteract this by remembering that you really don't know, that you really could be back smoking again. All you can ever do is not smoke just for now. This way of thinking keeps you in a genuine state of free choice. Then, you can stay in touch with what your choices are and what choices you really want to make.

- *Review this book* from time to time, even after you've stopped for a while. You could simply open the book at random every now and then, and read a page or two, just to keep in touch with these ideas.

- *If you still haven't set a quit date,* don't wait for life to be perfect before you try to quit. It won't be! And don't wait for your fear of failure to turn into confidence. It won't! At least, it won't until you face your fear, make a start on quitting and manage not to smoke for a while. Confidence can only come in time, after you've met some challenges, experienced strong feelings of temptation, lived through them and not smoked. Then, you can look back and say, 'So far, so good. I hope it stays this way. Let's see if I can keep going.'

How I Quit: Wendy

It comes and goes, and some days get quite difficult. Some days there have been quite strong desires. I was sitting in a café the other day, and out of the corner of my eye I saw that there was a cigarette machine. That brought back loads of memories of the times when I had gone into places with my money and bought cigarettes from those machines. Especially happy memories from university, when we would all gather around the cigarette machine in the student union bar. The desire came with quite a force when I saw that.

I've spent a bit of time over the past few weeks with a friend who smokes and I have quite a history of smoking with her. On the whole that's been OK, but there have been those odd moments, such as when we had a meal and she lit up a cigarette and I really, really wanted one. But the moment went quite quickly.

I had my cigarettes with me so I knew I could have one, but I thought it isn't going to just be one. After dinner, she's going to carry on smoking. So I try to reason with myself, 'OK, one cigarette would be absolutely wonderful, but it wouldn't stop there.'

When I smoked, I'd been on 20 a day for many years and then crept up to 25 to 30 a day, and I never thought that would happen. So I realise that as the years go by, if I did go back to smoking it could creep up to 40 or 50 a day. And I really don't want that. So as long as I can reason with myself like that, I'm going to be OK.

It's very easy for me to glorify smoking and to think that being a smoker was part of 'the good old days'. I know I need to be particularly careful on that one, and it's good for me to remember that my desire to smoke is nothing but a temporarily uncomfortable sensation and nothing more. I'm not playing the martyr and I'm not missing out on something unbelievably amazing, because just about everybody I know wants to give up, and if it was that amazing they wouldn't want to. I wake up in the morning and for a moment I forget, and then I think, 'Oh, I've stopped', and it's so exciting I can hardly believe it.

I'd been smoking for 16 years and have stopped for just a couple of weeks. It's weird, but it feels like I haven't had a cigarette for absolutely ages. Apparently a lot of people say that. I notice that for large chunks of the day I'm doing very well, so it's beginning to feel very natural for me not to smoke.

EVEN LAZIER

TOP 12 QUESTIONS – AND THE ANSWERS

1. **When will the cravings go?** It depends on what you mean by 'cravings'. I use the term 'desire to smoke' to mean any thought or feeling that could lead you to smoke. It could be a fleeting whim, an intense feeling of compulsion or anything in between these two extremes. As you know from Chapter 2, the desire becomes exaggerated when you feel deprived, and this is what I call a craving. When you genuinely choose, the sense of deprivation evaporates and you are left with more manageable thoughts of desire. So, the answer is that the cravings go when you genuinely connect with your freedom of choice. The desire remains, and after the first two days or so it gradually diminishes, both in frequency and in intensity.

2. **Won't I gain weight because my metabolism has slowed down when I've quit?** Studies which compare the metabolism of smokers and recent quitters show that there's very little change in metabolic rate as a result of stopping smoking. It could contribute to weight gain of a pound or two over some time, but no more. Most of the weight ex-smokers gain is through the substitution of food for cigarettes, although some people aren't aware they're eating more, so it's easy for them to assume their metabolism has been affected. Chapter 6 shows you how to identify and handle potential substitutions.

3. **Why is smoking such a health hazard?** Along with nicotine, each puff you inhale contains carbon monoxide, cyanide, arsenic, formaldehyde, acetone and carbolic acid, to name just a few of the poisons found in cigarette smoke. Carbon monoxide replaces the oxygen in your red blood cells, which is why smoking affects every part of the body. Every single cell is starved of oxygen. On top of this, about one cup of tar collects in your lungs every year. This onslaught causes the excess production of 'free radicals', damaged molecules which form the basis of the degenerative diseases. The aging process can be measured by the amount of free radicals in the body, which explains why smokers age faster than non-smokers, why they look older, wrinkle more, are more likely to become seriously ill and die as much as 20 years sooner than if they had quit. There is no such thing as a safe level of smoking and even passive smoking (breathing smoky air) has been shown to damage the health of non-smokers.

4. **How can I stop getting so terribly anxious when I quit smoking, and even just at the thought of quitting?** Each time you become aware that you're feeling anxious, you talk yourself through it by bringing yourself back into the here and now. If your anxiety starts before you've quit, think of quitting as something you'll try but you're not making any promises or commitments. It's the decision that once you've stopped, 'that will be it and you'll never smoke again' that's so negative. It's very possible that this thought alone will keep you smoking for the rest of your life! After you do quit, you say things like this

to yourself, 'Right now it's 4.30 in the afternoon on Tuesday, and so far so good. I'm not smoking, so up to now I've succeeded in quitting. I have no way of knowing if I'll keep it up and I can't possibly know whether or not I'll smoke in the future. I might smoke at some point later on, which means I'll be back smoking and I will have failed. Or, I might not. I've managed not to smoke so far and that's all I can do.' Anxiety always comes from your concern about what will happen in the future. Let go of your need to know about the future and your anxiety will go with it.

5. **Why do I get constipated when I quit and what can I do about it?** Smoking damages our bodies in so many ways. Most of this damage is unseen, so the health problems you experience – coughs, sore throats, low energy, difficulty waking up in the morning – are really the tip of an iceberg, so to speak. One area of unseen damage happens in our digestive systems, where the beneficial bacteria that help us to break down our food are killed off by nicotine (which can, by the way, be used as a pesticide). This would lead to constipation, but nicotine also has the effect of stimulating bowel movement. Most smokers are very aware of this, as their first cigarette of the day prompts a visit to the bathroom. So, when you've stopped smoking you're left without the artificial stimulation of the nicotine and depleted bacteria as well: thus the constipation. All you need to do is to visit your local health food shop and ask for products which replenish the bacteria. Lactobacillus Acidophilus is the most well-known (also added to some yoghurts available in the

supermarkets) but there are others, and nowadays there are quite a few products to choose from. As well as this, you can remedy constipation with plenty of water, exercise, aloe vera juice, linseeds (grind them in a coffee grinder and sprinkle on cereal), products containing psyllium husks, and many other items to be found at good health food stores.

6. **How can I quit if I'm physically addicted to nicotine?** Physical addiction means you experience physical withdrawal symptoms when you quit. These physical symptoms can be uncomfortable and even make you feel as if you are ill, but they are no more than signs that your body is detoxifying, recovering from being poisoned by tobacco smoke. The physical side of withdrawal from nicotine isn't all that intense and it's very temporary, lasting a day or two. However, the psychological withdrawal can be very difficult and prolonged if you are feeling deprived. The mental state of deprivation often creates physical symptoms of stress, such as tiredness, loss of concentration, tension and headaches. This gives the impression that physical addiction is the bigger problem, when in fact most of the difficulty is created by the 'victim' state of mind.

7. **When will I be able to get a good night's sleep after I quit?** Disturbed sleep is an added and unwelcome problem for many quitters. There could be three different causes for this sleeplessness, and so three different solutions. One cause may be that the body takes a while to adapt to increased energy, which can be quite dramatic even after one day of not

smoking. If you can use up a bit more energy in the day than you normally do, you may sleep better at night. A second cause comes from the stress, anxiety and tension that arises when you quit in a state of deprivation. Insomnia is a well-known symptom of stress, and a well-known source of stress is loss of freedom of choice. If you suspect this is behind your inability to sleep (especially if you are experiencing other symptoms of deprivation), Chapter 2 will help you to shift this, to bring down your level of stress from quitting and help you sleep through the night. The third cause is most likely if you have trouble falling asleep, rather than waking later on. It's often due to that fact that caffeine stays in the body for a longer period of time after you have stopped smoking. This means that if you drink anything with caffeine in it in the afternoon or evening, it will have a more lasting effect on you than when you smoked. This is especially true of coffee, which is very high in caffeine, and many soft drinks such as Coca Cola. Later on in the day, try drinking decaffeinated versions of your favourite drinks to see if your sleeping improves. By the way, if you are waking an hour or two earlier than you used to, this is not a problem but a benefit from quitting. It's possible you need less sleep now that you don't smoke. Why not use your extra hour to do something special for yourself?

8.   **What can I do if I just smoke one cigarette?** When a smoker quits and then smokes one cigarette or even just a puff or two, they may react in one of two ways. One is to think, 'Well, I've blown it now, so I'm back smoking,' and return to daily smoking

immediately. Alternatively, they feel shocked at what they've done and may not smoke again for days, weeks or in some cases even for months. Convinced they got away with it, smoking another cigarette is easier and much more compelling, so much so that at some point another is smoked, and another, and so on. This means that a return to smoking is more gradual but just as inevitable. A few people can manage to take control again after a relapse and succeed long term, but it's a very risky business. The key is to choose between accepting your desire to smoke or returning to a life of daily smoking. You're not doing that if you are smoking the odd cigarette here and there, and so the choice not to smoke gets almost impossible to make. By the way, this shows you that the main challenge in quitting is in your mind, rather than its being a matter of getting nicotine out of your body. You can get nicotine in your body through passive smoking, but this won't cause you to relapse. Much more dangerous is one little puff of a cigarette – even if you don't inhale it and even if you wait a few days before you take another puff.

9. **I really enjoy smoking; will I be able to quit?** You can, provided you see ways in which you will benefit from quitting. There needs to be something for you to gain as a result of quitting, so that you can get to a point where you can say, 'Yes, smoking is enjoyable, at least sometimes, but I like not smoking even more.' This is why it's crucial to make your own choices in this process. Otherwise, the feelings of deprivation can make quitting such a misery that you are strongly tempted back to smoking as a preferable way of life.

10. **Whenever I drink alcohol my willpower disappears – should I drink after I quit?** Yes, in fact I strongly recommend that you drink as soon as you normally would, even the same day you quit smoking. It's probably best not to get completely plastered, but sooner or later you'll be faced with that strong connection between smoking and drinking. When people say they lose their willpower when they drink, what happens is that drinking triggers a strong desire to smoke, which most people don't know how to handle. If you normally drink alcohol, it will be crucial for you to work through that desire to smoke, and the sooner you do that, the better. Make sure you don't use your inebriation as an excuse to smoke. You really can think in a responsible way, even when you're drunk, and make at least some wise decisions: about driving, for example, or getting home, or your sexual behaviour.

11. **I smoke marijuana and don't want to stop doing this at the present time. Will I still be able to quit smoking tobacco?** Yes, you certainly can. Be aware that the choice to smoke tobacco in any form is the choice to return to smoking, so always keep the two drugs separate. Be very careful not to substitute by keeping to your usual intake of marijuana. And of course remember that your desire to smoke tobacco will be strongly associated with smoking dope. Essentially, though, it's no different from wanting to smoke a cigarette with a glass of wine or beer.

12. **Is the damage I've done to myself through smoking reversible?** It's never too late to stop smoking. Your body begins to repair

itself and recover as soon as you quit, and within a half-hour your circulation, blood pressure and heart rate start to improve. The first thing you may notice is you have warmer hands and feet, especially in colder weather. By the first 24 hours, the amount of oxygen in your bloodstream becomes normal and there's no nicotine left in your body. Depending on the amount of smoking you've done, it can take three or four days before you notice an improvement in your breathing and energy, and even six months before your smoker's cough clears up. By one year, your risk of heart disease is half that of a smoker and by ten years it's the same as if you had never smoked. Even if you've already had a heart attack, quitting eases any ongoing pain and lessens your chance of having another. Risk of lung cancer falls gradually from the moment you stop, to about half that of a smoker in 10 years. Your body has an extraordinary ability to restore itself. Quitting at any age, even if you're in your 60s or 70s, increases the years in your life and the life in your years!

RESOURCES

■ You can call the free national Quitline on 0800 00 22 00 for someone to talk to about quitting smoking. It could be invaluable to talk through your experiences with someone who will listen, but please know that the advice you receive may not be entirely consistent with the approach described in this book.

■ Your local health authority, hospital or doctor's surgery may hold smoking cessation clinics and may also be able to provide you with telephone counselling.

■ ASH (Action on Smoking and Health) does excellent work to counteract the power of the tobacco industry, so please support this organisation in any way you can. Their web site at *www.ash.org.uk* is well worth a visit.

■ For a copy of my audio cassette in which I talk you through the techniques in this book, send a cheque (made out to me) for Stg£7.50 to: Gillian Riley, Full Stop, PO Box 2484, London N6 5UX.

READING GUIDE

■ *The Six Pillars of Self-Esteem* (Bantam, 1994) by Nathaniel Branden is the book I most frequently recommend to my clients. If you think self-esteem is an issue for you, it's well worth investing in this book, perhaps reading it on and off for years, as I do, and especially working on the exercises.

- *Mind Sculpture* (Bantam, 1999) by Ian Robertson provides you with more information on how our brains change physically with what we do and think, which we explored briefly in Chapter 7. One of the world's leading researchers on brain rehabilitation, Ian Robertson is a professor at Trinity College, Dublin and University College, London.

- *Beating overeating: The Lazy Person's Guide* (Newleaf, 2001) by Gillian Riley will take you through a similar process to that in *Quitting Smoking*, especially helpful for those who have a strong connection between food and smoking.

- *How to Stop Smoking and Stay Stopped for Good* (Vermilion, 1992) by Gillian Riley covers similar ground to Quitting Smoking, but is quite a bit longer. You might find it helpful to read about some of the issues in more detail.